# ZUMBARONS

## A FANTASY LAND OF MACARONS

## ADRIANO ZUMBO

MURDOCH BOOKS

# CONTENTS

# INTRODUCTION

**MACARONS BECAME MY PASSION** when I was working in a French patisserie in Sydney and my boss returned from a holiday in France with a 10-pack of Pierre Hermé macarons. They were unbelievable and unlike any I had tasted previously — soft and delicate with a smooth, crisp outer shell. What's more, they really tasted like the flavours they were named after. I dedicated two years to finding the perfect macaron recipe, then many more years to experimenting with flavours and textures.

This book features a selection of my favourite macarons, as well as some filling techniques that we have come up with at the Zumbo kitchen. I have included recipes for three different types of macaron shells: Italian, Swiss and French. The Italian meringue is the kind I use in my shops and is easiest to handle. The Swiss is a little more difficult and the original French meringue is the hardest to master. Try them all and see which you prefer.

I have also included some recipes for using macarons in desserts so you can experiment with combinations, textures and flavours.

The only limit is your imagination!

# MEET THE

**BEETROOT
RASPBERRY**

**BLACKENED
VANILLA BEAN**

**STRAWBERRY
BUBBLEGU**

**START** →

**CHERRY
COCONUT**

**CHOC
MAYONNAISE**

**EUCALYPTUS**

**CITRON**

**LICORICE**

**GIN & TONIC**

**GINGERBREAD
HOUSE**

**KALAMATA OLI**

# ZUMBARONS

**SALTED BUTTER POPCORN**

**PANDAN COCONUT**

**PANCAKE & MAPLE SYRUP**

**ROSE**

**MANDARIN**

**SALTED GIANDUJA CARAMEL**

**PEACH ICED TEA**

**PISTACHIO**

**STICKY DATE**

**SATAY**

**HOT X BUNS**

**BLUEBERRY LAVENDER**

**TOASTED MARSHMALLOW**

**CHOCOLATE PEANUT BUTTER & JELLY**

**CARAMEL AU BEURRE SALÉ**

**WASABI & PICKLED GINGER**

**VEGEMITE**

**FIG, BURNT HONEY & RED WINE**

**CHOCOLATE MARSHMALLOW LOLLIPOP**

**CONTD.→**

# PANCAKE & MAPLE SYRUP

## PANCAKE

30 g (1 oz) plain
  (all-purpose) flour
10 g (¼ oz) caster
  (superfine) sugar
0.25 g (¹⁄₅₀ oz) baking
  powder
38 g (1¹⁄₃ oz) milk
1 x 60 g (2¼ oz) egg,
  separated, at room
  temperature

## PANCAKE MAPLE SYRUP
## GANACHE

100 g (3½ oz) maple syrup
1 pancake (see recipe above)
120 g (4¼ oz) thin (pouring/
  whipping) cream (35% fat)
Seeds scraped from
  ½ vanilla bean
200 g (7 oz) white
  couverture chocolate,
  chopped or buttons

1 quantity macaron
  shells (see page 98),
  coloured beige

**MAKES 50**

To make the pancake, put the dry ingredients in a medium bowl. Lightly whisk the milk and egg yolk in a jug, then slowly whisk into the dry ingredients until well incorporated and smooth. Put the egg white in an electric mixer fitted with a whisk attachment and whisk until stiff peaks form. Gently fold the egg white into the pancake batter.

Lightly grease a small non-stick frying pan with butter or oil and heat over medium heat. Pour in the pancake batter and cook until bubbles begin to form on the surface, then turn and cook for a further 1–2 minutes. Transfer to a bowl.

To make the pancake maple syrup ganache, pour the maple syrup over the pancake and set aside for 1½ hours.

Put the cream and vanilla seeds in a saucepan over medium heat and bring to the boil. Put the chocolate in a bowl. Pour over the hot cream mixture and set aside for 2 minutes. Stir until smooth.

Blitz the pancake mixture with a stick mixer until smooth, then stir through the chocolate mixture. Allow the ganache to cool and become firm enough to pipe.

Fill a piping (icing) bag with a 7 mm (³⁄₈ inch) plain nozzle with the ganache. Pipe the ganache on the flat side of half the macaron shells, then top with the remaining shells. Put the assembled macarons in the refrigerator for 24 hours to set, then bring to room temperature and serve or transfer to an airtight container.

# RICE PUDDING

**MAKES 50**

To make the rice pudding, put all the ingredients in a saucepan over medium–low heat and cook until the rice is tender. Stir often to prevent the rice sticking on the base of the pan and add small amounts of additional milk if the mixture becomes too dry before the rice is cooked. Remove from the heat and allow to cool completely.

Meanwhile, to make the ganache, put the cream, vanilla seeds and cinnamon in a saucepan over medium heat and bring to the boil. Put the chocolate in a bowl. Pour over the hot cream and set aside for 2 minutes. Stir until smooth, then cool the mixture to 50°C (122°F).

When the chocolate mixture is at the right temperature, blitz in the butter with a stick mixer until smooth. Set the ganache aside to cool.

Put the ganache and rice pudding in a bowl and mix until combined. Fill a piping (icing) bag with a 12 mm (½ inch) plain nozzle with the rice pudding ganache. Pipe the ganache on the flat side of half the macaron shells, then top with the remaining shells. Put the assembled macarons in the refrigerator for 24 hours to set, then bring to room temperature and serve or transfer to an airtight container.

### RICE PUDDING
188 g (6¾ oz) thin (pouring/whipping) cream (35% fat)
188 g (6¾ oz) milk
75 g (2¾ oz) brown sugar
70 g (2½ oz) arborio or jasmine rice
50 g (1¾ oz) caster (superfine) sugar
6 g (⅕ oz) natural vanilla extract

### GANACHE
58 g (2¼ oz) thin (pouring/whipping) cream (35% fat)
Small pinch of seeds scraped from a vanilla bean
Small pinch of ground cinnamon
95 g (3¼ oz) white couverture chocolate, chopped or buttons
30 g (1 oz) unsalted butter, chopped and softened

1 quantity macaron shells (see page 98), sprinkled with ground cinnamon

3  RISE&SHINE

# PASSIONFRUIT

200 g (7 oz) lightly
  beaten egg
190 g (6¾ oz) caster
  (superfine) sugar
150 g (5½ oz) fresh
  passionfruit juice (see Note)
15 g (½ oz) fresh lemon juice
300 g (10½ oz) unsalted
  butter, chopped and
  softened

1 quantity macaron
  shells (see page 98),
  coloured dark purple

**MAKES 50**

Put the egg and sugar in a saucepan and stir well. Stir in
the passionfruit and lemon juices. Heat over medium to
low heat, stirring constantly, until the mixture reaches 85°C
(185°F). Strain the curd into a bowl, then cool to 50°C (122°F).

When the curd is at the right temperature, blitz in the
butter with a stick mixer until smooth and shiny. Allow the
curd to cool and become firm enough to pipe.

Fill a piping (icing) bag with a 7 mm (⅜ inch) plain nozzle
with the curd. Pipe the curd on the flat side of half the
macaron shells, then top with the remaining shells. Put the
assembled macarons in the refrigerator for 24 hours to set,
then bring to room temperature and serve or transfer to
an airtight container.

**NOTE:** To make fresh passionfruit juice, scoop out the
pulp into a sieve set over a bowl. Press down on the pulp
with a spoon to extract all the juice. You will need about
7 passionfruit to produce the required amount.

The curd must be stirred constantly as it cooks to avoid
ending up with scrambled eggs.

To make passionfruit & basil macarons, infuse the
passionfruit juice with 20 g (¾ oz) shredded basil leaves
for 30 minutes. Strain the juice to remove the basil before
making the curd.

To make passionfruit & tonka bean macarons, stir a finely
grated tonka bean (see Glossary) through the curd after
blitzing in the butter.

# VEGEMITE

**MAKES 50**

Put the cream in a saucepan over medium heat and bring to the boil. Put the chocolate and Vegemite in a bowl. Pour over the hot cream and set aside for 2 minutes. Stir until the mixture is smooth. Stir in the breadcrumbs, then cool the mixture to 50°C (122°F).

When the chocolate mixture is at the right temperature, blitz in the butter with a stick mixer until smooth. Allow the ganache to cool and become firm enough to pipe.

Fill a piping (icing) bag with a 9 mm (⅓ inch) plain nozzle with the ganache. Pipe the ganache on the flat side of half the macaron shells, then top with the remaining shells. Put the assembled macarons in the refrigerator for 24 hours to set, then bring to room temperature and serve or transfer to an airtight container.

188 g (6¾ oz) thin (pouring/whipping) cream (35% fat)
225 g (8 oz) white couverture chocolate, chopped or buttons
40 g (1½ oz) Vegemite™
50 g (1¾ oz) fresh breadcrumbs, toasted
125 g (4½ oz) unsalted butter, chopped and softened

1 quantity macaron shells (see page 98), coloured light brown

# HOT X BUNS

¼ hot cross bun

½ hot cross bun, soaked in lukewarm water for 3 minutes, then drained

120 g (4¼ oz) thin (pouring/ whipping) cream (35% fat)

0.5 g (¹⁄₅₀ oz) ground cloves

0.25 g (¹⁄₅₀ oz) ground allspice

0.15 g (¹⁄₅₀ oz) ground cardamom

160 g (5½ oz) white couverture chocolate, chopped or buttons

40 g (1½ oz) unsalted butter, chopped and softened

20 g (¾ oz) candied orange peel, finely chopped

20 g (¾ oz) raisins, soaked in hot water for 30 minutes, then drained and roughly chopped

1 quantity macaron shells (see page 98), coloured light brown (see Note)

**MAKES 50**

Cut the hot cross bun quarter into 3 slices. Leave on a tray, covered with a cloth, to dry out overnight.

Process the dried hot cross bun to coarse breadcrumbs and transfer to a small bowl. Drain the water from the other hot cross bun, then process to a purée.

Put the cream and spices in a saucepan over medium heat and bring to the boil. Put the chocolate in a bowl. Pour over the hot cream mixture and set aside for 2 minutes. Stir until smooth, then cool the mixture to 50°C (122°F).

When the chocolate mixture is at the right temperature, blitz in the butter with a stick mixer until smooth. Fold through the orange peel, hot cross bun purée and crumbs, and chopped raisins. Allow the ganache to cool and become firm enough to pipe.

Fill a piping (icing) bag with a 7 mm (³⁄₈ inch) plain nozzle with the ganache. Pipe the ganache on the flat side of half the macaron shells, then top with the remaining shells. Put the assembled macarons in the refrigerator for 24 hours to set, then bring to room temperature and serve or transfer to an airtight container.

**NOTE:** To make the crosses on the shells, you will need some uncoloured macaron mixture. As soon as you pipe each macaron onto the tray, pipe a cross on top using the uncoloured mixture. Don't pipe all the way to the edge — when you tap the tray the lines will extend.

# MANDARIN

**MAKES 50**

Put the cream in a saucepan over medium heat and bring to the boil. Put the chocolate in a bowl. Pour over the hot cream and set aside for 2 minutes. Stir until smooth, then cool to 50°C (122°F).

Meanwhile, heat the mandarin purée in a small saucepan over medium heat until it reaches 60°C (140°F). When the chocolate mixture is at the right temperature, stir in the 60°C purée until combined. Allow the ganache to cool and become firm enough to pipe.

Fill a piping (icing) bag with a 7 mm (⅜ inch) plain nozzle with the ganache. Pipe the ganache on the flat side of half the macaron shells, then top with the remaining shells. Put the assembled macarons in the refrigerator for 24 hours to set, then bring to room temperature and serve or transfer to an airtight container.

**NOTE:** To make mandarin & tonka bean macarons, add a finely grated tonka bean (see Glossary) to the chocolate mixture when adding the mandarin purée.

To make mandarin & saffron macarons, add 0.5 g (¹/₅₀ oz) saffron threads to the cream before bringing it to the boil.

100 g (3½ oz) thin (pouring/whipping) cream (35% fat)
540 g (1 lb 3 oz) white couverture chocolate, chopped or buttons
440 g (15½ oz) mandarin purée (see page 105)

1 quantity macaron shells (see page 98), coloured orange

# CHOCOLATE PEANUT BUTTER & JELLY

## JELLY

125 g (4½ oz) redcurrant
  purée (see page 105)
125 g (4½ oz) raspberry
  purée (see page 105)
62 g (2¼ oz) caster
  (superfine) sugar
1.5 g (¹⁄₂₀ oz) gellan
  (see Glossary)
1 g (¹⁄₂₅ oz) iota (see Glossary)

*contd ››*

**MAKES 50**

To make the jelly, put the redcurrant and raspberry purées, sugar, gellan and iota in a saucepan and blitz with a stick mixer until smooth and thickened slightly. Bring the mixture to the boil over medium heat, then pour into a square 12 cm (4½ inch) container. Refrigerate until set, then cut into 1.5 cm (⅝ inch) squares.

To make the chocolate & peanut butter ganache, put the cream in a saucepan over medium heat and bring to the boil. Put the chocolate in a bowl. Pour over the hot cream and set aside for 2 minutes. Add the peanut butter and stir until smooth, then bring the mixture to 50°C (122°F).

When the chocolate mixture is at the right temperature, blitz in the butter with a stick mixer until smooth. Fold through the sea salt. Allow the ganache to cool and become firm enough to pipe.

Fill a piping (icing) bag with a 9 mm (⅓ inch) plain nozzle with the ganache. Pipe the ganache on the flat side of the chocolate macaron shells, then press a piece of jelly into the centre of the ganache on each macaron. Top with the red macaron shells. Put the assembled macarons in the refrigerator for 24 hours to set, then bring to room temperature and serve or transfer to an airtight container.

## CHOCOLATE & PEANUT BUTTER GANACHE

100 g (3½ oz) thin (pouring/whipping) cream (35% fat)
240 g (8½ oz) milk couverture chocolate, chopped or buttons
215 g (7½ oz) crunchy peanut butter
50 g (1¾ oz) unsalted butter, chopped and softened
1 g (¹⁄₂₅ oz) sea salt flakes

½ quantity chocolate macaron shells (see page 98)
½ quantity macaron shells (see page 98), coloured red

# GARDEN of EDEN

# CHERRY COCONUT

## CHERRY JELLY

6 g (⅕ oz) gold gelatine
   leaves (see Glossary)
36 g (1¼ oz) cold water
250 g (9 oz) cherry purée
   (see page 105)
50 g (1¾ oz) caster
   (superfine) sugar

## CHERRY & COCONUT GANACHE

132 g (4⅔ oz) UHT coconut
   cream (see Glossary)
180 g (6¼ oz) milk
   couverture chocolate,
   chopped or buttons
48 g (1¾ oz) unsalted butter,
   chopped and softened
30 g (1 oz) desiccated
   coconut

1 quantity macaron shells
   (see page 98), coloured
   cherry red and sprinkled
   with desiccated coconut

**MAKES 50**

To make the cherry jelly, cut the gelatine into small squares, combine with the water and set aside to soak.

Put one-quarter of the cherry purée in a saucepan over medium heat, add the sugar and heat to 50°C (122°F). Stir in the gelatine, including any soaking liquid, and stir well to ensure all the gelatine dissolves. Add the remaining cherry purée and mix well.

Pour the jelly mixture into a square 12 cm (4½ inch) container. Put in the refrigerator until set, then cut the jelly into 1.5 cm (⅝ inch) squares.

To make the cherry & coconut ganache, put the coconut cream in a saucepan over medium heat and bring to the boil. Put the chocolate in a bowl. Pour over the hot coconut cream and set aside for 2 minutes. Stir until smooth, then cool the mixture to 50°C (122°F).

When the chocolate mixture is at the right temperature, blitz in the butter with a stick mixer until smooth. Fold through the coconut. Allow the ganache to cool and become firm enough to pipe.

Fill a piping (icing) bag with a 9 mm (⅓ inch) plain nozzle with the ganache. Pipe onto the flat side of half the macaron shells, then gently press a piece of cherry jelly into the centre of each. Top with the remaining macaron shells. Put the assembled macarons in the refrigerator for 24 hours to set, then bring to room temperature and serve or transfer to an airtight container.

# BANANA

**MAKES 50**

330 g (11½ oz) ripe bananas, peeled and chopped
10 g (¼ oz) fresh lemon juice
82 g (2¾ oz) thin (pouring/ whipping) cream (35% fat)
510 g (1 lb 2¼ oz) white couverture chocolate, chopped or buttons

1 quantity macaron shells (see page 98), coloured yellow

Purée the banana and lemon juice in a food processor until smooth.

Put the cream and banana purée in a saucepan over medium heat and bring to the boil. Put the chocolate in a bowl. Pour over the hot cream mixture and set aside for 2 minutes. Stir until smooth. Allow the ganache to cool and become firm enough to pipe.

Fill a piping (icing) bag with a 7 mm (⅜ inch) plain nozzle with the ganache. Pipe the ganache on the flat side of half the macaron shells, then top with the remaining shells. Put the assembled macarons in the refrigerator for 24 hours to set, then bring to room temperature and serve or transfer to an airtight container.

**NOTE:** To make banana mustard macarons, add the seeds scraped from 1 vanilla bean to the cream and banana purée before heating and pouring over the chocolate. Stir 100 g (3½ oz) dijon mustard and 100 g (3½ oz) wholegrain mustard into the ganache before leaving it to cool and firm.

# LYCHEE

## LYCHEE GEL

180 g (6¼ oz) lychee purée
  (see page 105)
22.5 g (¾ oz) liquid glucose
42 g (1½ oz) caster
  (superfine) sugar
3.5 g (⅛ oz) pectin NH
  (see Glossary)
2 g (²⁄₂₅ oz) citric acid
  solution (see page 105)

## LYCHEE CUSTRIANO

58 g (2¼ oz) caster
  (superfine) sugar
6 g (⅕ oz) iota
  (see Glossary)
2.5 g (²⁄₂₅ oz) kappa
  (see Glossary)
600 g (1 lb 5 oz) lychee
  purée (see page 105)
390 g (13¾ oz) thin (pouring/
  whipping) cream (35% fat)

*contd* ››

**MAKES 50**

To make the lychee gel, put the lychee purée and glucose in a saucepan and heat to 60°C (140°F). Put the sugar and pectin in a small bowl and mix well.

When the lychee mixture is at the right temperature, whisk in the pectin mixture. Bring to the boil and boil for 30 seconds, then add the citric acid solution and remove from the heat. Stir and then cool to room temperature.

To make the lychee custriano, put the sugar, iota and kappa in a small bowl. Put the lychee purée and cream in a saucepan. Add the sugar mixture and blitz with a stick mixer until well combined. Bring to the boil and boil for 1 minute. Remove from the heat, pour into a bowl and cover with plastic wrap, pressing it onto the surface to prevent a skin forming. Refrigerate overnight.

To make the lychee custriano filling, put 250 g (9 oz) of the custriano in an electric mixer fitted with a whisk attachment. Whisk on medium speed, slowly adding the butter until it is all incorporated. Blend 100 g (3½ oz) of the lychee gel in a food processor briefly, then fold it through the custriano.

Fill a piping (icing) bag with a 7 mm (⅜ inch) plain nozzle with the lychee custriano filling. Pipe the filling on the flat side of half the macaron shells, then top with the remaining shells. Put the assembled macarons in the refrigerator for 24 hours to set, then bring to room temperature and serve or transfer to an airtight container.

### LYCHEE CUSTRIANO FILLING

250 g (9 oz) lychee custriano (see recipe opposite)

100 g (3½ oz) unsalted butter, chopped and softened

100 g (3½ oz) lychee gel (see recipe opposite)

1 quantity macaron shells (see page 98), coloured white by mixing a little food colouring powder with a tiny bit of water and adding to the sugar syrup, and sprinkled with red lentils blitzed to crumbs

# PANDAN COCONUT

150 g (5½ oz) UHT coconut cream (see Glossary)

5 g (⅛ oz) pandan extract (see Glossary)

2 pandan leaves (see Glossary)

1 kaffir lime leaf, chopped

250 g (9 oz) white couverture chocolate, chopped or buttons

80 g (2¾ oz) unsalted butter, chopped and softened

15 g (½ oz) desiccated coconut

1 quantity macaron shells (see page 98), coloured white by mixing a little food colouring powder with a tiny bit of water and adding to the sugar syrup, and topped with shredded coconut, coloured green (see Note)

**MAKES 50**

Put the coconut cream, pandan extract, pandan leaves and kaffir lime leaf in a saucepan over medium heat and bring to the boil. Turn off the heat and set aside for 20 minutes to infuse. Process in a food processor to break up the leaves so they release more flavour, then strain. Discard the leaves.

Return the cream mixture to the boil. Put the chocolate in a bowl. Pour over the hot cream mixture and set aside for 2 minutes. Stir until smooth, then cool to 50°C (122°F).

When the chocolate mixture is at the right temperature, blitz in the butter with a stick mixer until smooth. Fold in the desiccated coconut. Allow the ganache to cool and become firm enough to pipe.

Fill a piping (icing) bag with a 9 mm (⅓ inch) plain nozzle with the ganache. Pipe the ganache on the flat side of half the macaron shells, then top with the remaining shells. Put the assembled macarons in the refrigerator for 24 hours to set, then bring to room temperature and serve or transfer to an airtight container.

**NOTE:** To colour the coconut, put it in a plastic bag with a few drops of green food colouring, seal and shake well.

# PEACH ICED TEA

**MAKES 50**

To make the tea jelly, put the pectin and half the sugar in a small bowl and mix well. Put the peach purée, tea, gellan and the remaining sugar in a small saucepan over medium heat and cook until the mixture reaches 60°C (140°F).

When the peach mixture is at the right temperature, whisk in the pectin mixture. Bring to the boil and boil, stirring, for 30 seconds. Pour into a square 10 cm (4 inch) container and leave until set. Cut into 2 x 1 cm (¾ x ½ inch) pieces.

To make the peach iced tea ganache, put the cream and tea leaves in a saucepan over medium heat and bring to the boil. Put the chocolate in a bowl. Strain over the hot cream, discarding the tea leaves, and set aside for 2 minutes. Stir until smooth.

Put the peach purée in a saucepan and heat to 60°C (140°F), then stir into the chocolate mixture. Allow the ganache to cool and become firm enough to pipe. Transfer a quarter of the ganache to a separate bowl and reserve.

Fill a piping (icing) bag with a 7 mm (⅜ inch) plain nozzle with the remaining ganache. Pipe the ganache on the flat side of half the macaron shells. Press a piece of tea jelly into the centre of each, then pipe the reserved ganache over to cover the jelly. Top with the remaining shells. Put the assembled macarons in the refrigerator for 24 hours to set, then bring to room temperature and serve or transfer to an airtight container.

**NOTE:** Make a strong infusion of English breakfast tea, then strain and measure out 13 g (⅖ oz) of liquid.

## TEA JELLY

4 g (⅛ oz) pectin NH (see Glossary)
20 g (¾ oz) caster (superfine) sugar
200 g (7 oz) peach purée (see page 105)
13 g (⅖ oz) English breakfast tea (see Note)
0.8 g (¹⁄₂₅ oz) gellan (see Glossary)

## PEACH ICED TEA GANACHE

150 g (5½ oz) thin (pouring/ whipping) cream (35% fat)
22 g (¾ oz) English breakfast tea leaves
495 g (1 lb 2 oz) white couverture chocolate, chopped or buttons
150 g (5½ oz) peach purée (see page 105)

1 quantity macaron shells (see page 98), coloured peach and sprinkled with English breakfast tea leaves

# BLUEBERRY LAVENDER

75 g (2¾ oz) thin (pouring/ whipping) cream (35% fat)
4.5 g (³⁄₂₀ oz) dried culinary lavender flowers
250 g (9 oz) white couverture chocolate, chopped or buttons
75 g (2¾ oz) blueberry purée (see page 105)
1 quantity macaron shells (see page 98), coloured dusty lavender with flecks of blue (see Note)

**MAKES 50**

Put the cream and lavender flowers in a saucepan over medium heat and bring to the boil. Turn off the heat and set aside for 30 minutes to infuse.

Return the cream to the boil. Put the chocolate in a bowl. Strain the hot cream over and set aside for 2 minutes. Stir until smooth.

Heat the blueberry purée in a saucepan over medium heat until it reaches 60°C (140°F). Add to the chocolate mixture and mix well. Allow the ganache to cool and become firm enough to pipe.

Fill a piping (icing) bag with a 7 mm (⅜ inch) plain nozzle with the ganache. Pipe the ganache on the flat side of half the macaron shells, then top with the remaining shells. Put the assembled macarons in the refrigerator for 24 hours to set, then bring to room temperature and serve or transfer to an airtight container.

**NOTE:** To make the blue flecks, dip a pastry brush in blue food colouring and flick over each macaron shell.

# CHOCOLATE ORANGE

**MAKES 50**

Put the cream and orange zest in a saucepan over medium heat and bring to the boil. Put the chocolate in a bowl. Pour over the hot cream and set aside for 2 minutes. Stir until smooth, then cool to 50°C (122°F).

When the chocolate mixture is at the right temperature, blitz in the butter with a stick mixer until smooth. Allow the ganache to cool and become firm enough to pipe.

Fill a piping (icing) bag with a 7 mm (⅜ inch) plain nozzle with the ganache. Pipe the ganache on the flat side of half the macaron shells, then top with the remaining shells. Put the assembled macarons in the refrigerator for 24 hours to set, then bring to room temperature and serve or transfer to an airtight container.

150 g (5½ oz) thin (pouring/whipping) cream (35% fat)

Finely grated zest of 2 oranges

200 g (7 oz) milk couverture chocolate, chopped or buttons

60 g (2¼ oz) unsalted butter, chopped and softened

1 quantity macaron shells (see page 98), coloured orange and dusted with unsweetened cocoa powder

# CITRON

**MAKES 50**

160 g (5½ oz) lightly beaten
  egg, at room temperature
240 g (8½ oz) caster
  (superfine) sugar
Finely grated zest of
  5 lemons
160 g (5½ oz) strained
  freshly squeezed
  lemon juice
300 g (10½ oz) unsalted
  butter, chopped and
  softened

1 quantity macaron
  shells (see page 98),
  coloured yellow

Put the egg and sugar in a saucepan and mix well. Stir in the lemon zest and juice. Heat over medium to low heat, stirring constantly, until the mixture reaches 85°C (185°F). Strain the curd into a bowl, discarding the lemon zest, then cool to 50°C (122°F).

When the curd is at the right temperature, blitz in the butter with a stick mixer until smooth and shiny. Allow the curd to cool and become firm enough to pipe.

Fill a piping (icing) bag with a 7 mm (⅜ inch) plain nozzle with the curd. Pipe the curd on the flat side of half the macaron shells, then top with the remaining shells. Put the assembled macarons in the refrigerator for 24 hours to set, then bring to room temperature and serve or transfer to an airtight container.

**NOTE:** The curd must be stirred constantly as it cooks to avoid ending up with scrambled eggs.

# BEETROOT RASPBERRY

**MAKES 50**

To make the raspberry jelly, combine the pectin NH, gellan and sugar in a small bowl. Put the raspberry purée in a saucepan over medium heat and bring to 50°C (122°F). Add the sugar mixture and mix well. Bring to the boil, then boil for 1 minute. Pour into a square 12 cm (4½ inch) container. Refrigerate until set, then cut into 1.5 cm (⅝ inch) squares.

To make the beetroot buttercream, put the sugar and water in a small saucepan over medium heat and bring to the boil. Whisk in the beetroot powder. Boil the sugar syrup until it reaches 118°C (244°F).

Meanwhile, put the egg and egg yolks in an electric mixer with a whisk attachment and whisk on medium speed for 2 minutes. With the motor running, slowly pour the hot sugar syrup in a thin steady stream over the egg. Continue mixing until thick and cooled to 30°C (86°F). Slowly add the butter, a cube at a time, mixing well. It may appear curdled, but continue mixing until it is creamy and thick enough to pipe.

Fill a piping (icing) bag with a 7 mm (⅜ inch) plain nozzle with the buttercream. Pipe onto the flat side of half the macaron shells. Press a piece of raspberry jelly into the centre of each, then top with the remaining shells. Put the assembled macarons in the refrigerator for 24 hours to set, then bring to room temperature and serve or transfer to an airtight container.

## RASPBERRY JELLY

- 3 g (1⁄10 oz) pectin NH (see Glossary)
- 1 g (1⁄25 oz) gellan (see Glossary)
- 13 g (½ oz) caster (superfine) sugar
- 125 g (4½ oz) raspberry purée (see page 105)

## BEETROOT BUTTERCREAM

- 100 g (3½ oz) caster (superfine) sugar
- 38 g (1⅓ oz) water
- 5 g (⅛ oz) freeze-dried beetroot powder (see Glossary)
- 75 g (2¾ oz) lightly beaten egg
- 45 g (1¾ oz) egg yolks
- 200 g (7 oz) unsalted butter, chopped and softened

1 quantity macaron shells (see page 98), coloured red

# TEA PARTY

# CHOC MAYONNAISE

## MAYONNAISE SUSPENSION

175 g (6 oz) Japanese mayonnaise (see Glossary)
3 g (¹⁄₁₀ oz) xanthan gum (see Glossary)

## CHOCOLATE & MAYONNAISE GANACHE

38 g (1¹⁄₃ oz) thin (pouring/whipping) cream (35% fat)
38 g (1¹⁄₃ oz) raspberry purée (see page 105)
225 g (8 oz) dark couverture chocolate (64%), chopped or buttons
175 g (6 oz) mayonnaise suspension (see recipe above)
88 g (3¹⁄₄ oz) unsalted butter, chopped and softened

1 quantity chocolate macaron shells (see page 98), dusted with edible silver metallic (see Glossary)

**MAKES 50**

To make the mayonnaise suspension, whisk together the mayonnaise and xanthan gum.

To make the chocolate & mayonnaise ganache, put the cream and raspberry purée in a saucepan over medium heat and bring to the boil. Put the chocolate in a bowl. Pour over the hot cream mixture and set aside for 2 minutes. Stir until the mixture is smooth, then mix in 175 g (6 oz) of the mayonnaise suspension. Cool the mixture to 50°C (122°F).

When the chocolate mixture is at the right temperature, blitz in the butter with a stick mixer until smooth. Allow the ganache to cool and become firm enough to pipe.

Fill a piping (icing) bag with a 7 mm (³⁄₈ inch) plain nozzle with the ganache. Pipe the ganache on the flat side of half the macaron shells, then top with the remaining shells. Put the assembled macarons in the refrigerator for 24 hours to set, then bring to room temperature and serve or transfer to an airtight container.

# CARAMEL AU BEURRE SALÉ

**MAKES 50**

## CARAMEL MAISON

220 g (7¾ oz) thin (pouring/whipping) cream (35% fat)
1 vanilla bean, split lengthways and seeds scraped
120 g (4¼ oz) water
300 g (10½ oz) caster (superfine) sugar
60 g (2¼ oz) liquid glucose

## CARAMEL BUTTERCREAM

150 g (5½ oz) unsalted butter, chopped and softened
300 g (10½ oz) caramel maison (see recipe above)
4.5 g (³⁄₂₀ oz) sea salt flakes

1 quantity macaron shells (see page 98), coloured caramel

To make the caramel maison, put the cream and vanilla seeds and bean in a saucepan over medium heat. Bring to the boil, then remove from the heat and remove the vanilla bean.

Meanwhile, put the water, sugar and glucose in a heavy-based saucepan over medium–low heat and cook, stirring occasionally, until the sugar has dissolved. Brush down the side of the pan with a clean pastry brush dipped in water to avoid crystallisation. Increase the heat to medium and cook until a dark-amber colour. Carefully stir the hot cream mixture into the caramel to deglaze — watch out, it will spit and release a lot of heat. Stir until smooth. Transfer to a bowl and cool to 20°C (68°F).

To make the caramel buttercream, put the butter in an electric mixer and beat on medium speed until light and fluffy. With the electric mixer running, slowly add 300 g (10½ oz) of the warm caramel maison and continue mixing until thick and creamy. Fold through the sea salt.

Fill a piping (icing) bag with a 7 mm (³⁄₈ inch) plain nozzle with the buttercream. Pipe the buttercream on the flat side of half the macaron shells, then top with the remaining shells. Put the assembled macarons in the refrigerator for 24 hours to set, then bring to room temperature and serve or transfer to an airtight container.

**NOTE:** Cool the leftover caramel maison, then cover with plastic wrap and refrigerate. To use, heat in the microwave on medium (50%) until it reaches a pouring consistency (approximately 1 minute) and serve with vanilla ice cream.

# ROSE

**MAKES 50**

200 g (7 oz) thin (pouring/ whipping) cream (35% fat)

335 g (11¾ oz) white couverture chocolate, chopped or buttons

40 g (1½ oz) rosewater or rose extract

1 quantity macaron shells (see page 98), coloured deep pink

Put the cream in a saucepan over medium heat and bring to the boil. Put the chocolate in a bowl. Pour over the hot cream and set aside for 2 minutes. Stir until smooth. Stir through the rose compound. Allow the ganache to cool and become firm enough to pipe.

Fill a piping (icing) bag with a 7 mm (⅜ inch) plain nozzle with the ganache. Pipe the ganache on the flat side of half the macaron shells, then top with the remaining shells. Put the assembled macarons in the refrigerator for 24 hours to set, then bring to room temperature and serve or transfer to an airtight container.

# BLACKENED VANILLA BEAN

**MAKES 50**

To make the blackened vanilla bean dust, preheat the oven to 200°C (400°F/Gas 6). Put the vanilla beans on a baking tray and bake for approximately 30 minutes, until blackened, dry and crisp. Set aside to cool.

Put the cooled beans in a spice grinder and grind to a fine dust. This will make 15 g (½ oz) of dust.

To make the blackened vanilla crème, put the almond meal in a dry frying pan over medium heat and toast, stirring often, until light golden. Transfer to a bowl and allow to cool.

Put the butter and icing sugar in an electric mixer with a beater attachment. Beat on low speed until combined, then increase the speed to medium and continue to beat until pale and fluffy, approximately 4 minutes. Reduce the speed to low and add the toasted almond meal and 14 g (½ oz) of the blackened vanilla bean dust. Mix until just combined. Remove the bowl from the mixer and use a spatula or spoon to fold through the crème pâtissière.

Fill a piping (icing) bag with a 7 mm (⅜ inch) plain nozzle with the blackened vanilla crème. Pipe the crème on the flat side of half the macaron shells, then top with the remaining shells. Put the assembled macarons in the refrigerator for 24 hours to set, then bring to room temperature and serve or transfer to an airtight container.

## BLACKENED VANILLA BEAN DUST

6 large vanilla beans (30 g/1 oz in total)

## BLACKENED VANILLA CRÈME

150 g (5½ oz) almond meal
120 g (4¼ oz) unsalted butter, chopped and softened
120 g (4¼ oz) pure icing (confectioners') sugar
14 g (½ oz) blackened vanilla bean dust (see recipe above)
110 g (3¾ oz) crème pâtissière (see page 104), at room temperature

1 quantity macaron shells (see page 98), coloured black

# RASPBERRY SHORTBREAD

## SHORTBREAD

250 g (9 oz) unsalted butter,
    chopped and softened
125 g (4½ oz) raw
    (demerara) sugar
Seeds scraped from
    ½ vanilla bean
250 g (9 oz) plain
    (all-purpose) flour
125 g (4½ oz) rice flour

*contd ››*

### MAKES 50

To make the shortbread, put the butter, sugar and vanilla seeds in an electric mixer with a paddle attachment. Mix on medium speed until light and fluffy. Add the flours and mix until combined.

Place a sheet of plastic wrap on a work surface. Turn the dough out onto the plastic wrap, then fold it over the top and press down to a disc, about 2 cm (¾ inch) thick. Refrigerate for about 2 hours, until firm.

Meanwhile, to make the raspberry jam, put the pectin and a little of the sugar in a small bowl and mix well. Put the raspberry purée and the remaining sugar in a saucepan over medium heat and cook until it reaches 60°C (140°F) and the sugar has dissolved. Stir in the pectin mixture and bring to the boil. Whisk in the glucose and boil for 30 seconds, then add the citric acid solution. Stir and remove from the heat. Leave the jam out at room temperature for approximately 1 hour, until set (see Note).

Preheat the oven to 120°C (235°F/Gas ½). Line 2 large baking sheets with non-stick baking paper.

Lightly dust your work surface with flour and use a rolling pin to roll out the shortbread dough until 2 mm (¹⁄₁₆ inch) thick. Use a 4 cm (1½ inch) cutter to cut out 50 rounds.

Place the shortbread rounds on the lined trays and bake for about 50 minutes, until light golden. Remove from the oven and cool on the trays.

Fill a piping (icing) bag with a 7 mm (⅜ inch) plain nozzle with the raspberry jam. Pipe the jam on the flat side of half the macaron shells (only use about half the jam as you'll need the rest for the shortbread rounds). Place a shortbread round on top of each. Pipe another small amount of jam over the shortbread and top with the remaining macaron shells. Put the assembled macarons in the refrigerator for 24 hours to set, then bring to room temperature and serve or transfer to an airtight container.

**NOTE:** Jam usually sets at around 21–25°C (70–77°F).

### RASPBERRY JAM

7 g (¼ oz) pectin NH
(see Glossary)
84 g (3 oz) caster
(superfine) sugar
360 g (12¾ oz) raspberry
purée (see page 105)
45 g (1¾ oz) liquid glucose
4 g (⅛ oz) citric acid solution
(see page 105)

1 quantity macaron shells
(see page 98), coloured red

# LICORICE

**MAKES 50**

175 g (6 oz) thin (pouring/
whipping) cream (35% fat)
45 g (1¾ oz) soft licorice
(as fresh as possible),
chopped
250 g (9 oz) white
couverture chocolate,
chopped or buttons
80 g (2¾ oz) unsalted butter,
chopped and softened

1 quantity macaron
shells (see page 98),
coloured black

Put the cream and licorice in a saucepan over medium heat and bring to the boil. Remove from the heat and blitz the cream and licorice together with a stick mixer until smooth.

Put the chocolate in a bowl. Pour over the hot licorice cream and set aside for 2 minutes. Stir until smooth, then cool the mixture to 50°C (122°F).

When the mixture is at the right temperature, blitz in the butter with a stick mixer until smooth. Allow the ganache to cool and become firm enough to pipe.

Fill a piping (icing) bag with a 7 mm (⅜ inch) plain nozzle with the ganache. Pipe the ganache on the flat side of half the macaron shells, then top with the remaining shells. Put the assembled macarons in the refrigerator for 24 hours to set, then bring to room temperature and serve or transfer to an airtight container.

# SALTED GIANDUJA CARAMEL

**MAKES 50**

Put the cream and cocoa butter in a small saucepan over medium heat and bring to the boil.

Meanwhile, put the sugar in a deep saucepan over medium–low heat and shake the pan frequently until the sugar liquefies to ensure it doesn't burn. Cook, without stirring, until the syrup is caramelised and dark amber.

Pour the hot cream over the syrup and stir until smooth. Take care as the mixture will spit and release a lot of steam.

Put both chocolates in a large heatproof bowl. Pour over the hot caramel and set aside for 2 minutes. Stir until smooth, then cool the mixture to 50°C (122°F).

When the chocolate mixture is at the right temperature, blitz in the butter with a stick mixer until smooth. Fold through the salt. Allow the ganache to cool and become firm enough to pipe.

Fill a piping (icing) bag with a 7 mm (³⁄₈ inch) plain nozzle with the ganache. Pipe the ganache on the flat side of the chocolate macaron shells, then top with the light-brown shells. Put the assembled macarons in the refrigerator for 24 hours to set, then bring to room temperature and serve or transfer to an airtight container.

150 g (5½ oz) thin (pouring/whipping) cream (35% fat)

25 g (⁹⁄₁₀ oz) cocoa butter (see Glossary), finely chopped

125 g (4½ oz) caster (superfine) sugar

200 g (7 oz) gianduja chocolate (see Glossary), chopped

50 g (1¾ oz) milk couverture chocolate, chopped or buttons

80 g (2¾ oz) unsalted butter, chopped and softened

1 g (¹⁄₂₅ oz) sea salt flakes

½ quantity chocolate macaron shells (see page 98)

½ quantity macaron shells (see page 98), coloured light brown

# STICKY DATE

### DATE PURÉE

90 g (3¼ oz) stoned dates,
  chopped
2.5 g (²/₂₅ oz) bicarbonate of
  soda (baking soda)
150 g (5½ oz) boiling water

### STICKY DATE GANACHE

250 g (9 oz) white
  couverture chocolate,
  chopped or buttons
100 g (3½ oz) date purée
  (see recipe above)
38 g (1⅓ oz) thin (pouring/
  whipping) cream (35% fat)
30 g (1 oz) date molasses
  (see Glossary)
80 g (2¾ oz) unsalted butter,
  chopped and softened

*contd* ››

**MAKES 50**

To make the date purée, put the dates and bicarbonate of
soda in a bowl, pour over the boiling water and set aside for
20 minutes. Pour off the excess water, then purée the dates
in a food processor until smooth.

To make the sticky date ganache, melt the chocolate
in a heatproof bowl over a saucepan of simmering water
(make sure the base of the bowl doesn't touch the water)
or in the microwave on medium (50%) in 30-second
bursts, stirring after each burst. Take care not to burn the
chocolate as it will become grainy. Add 100 g (3½ oz) of
the date purée to the melted chocolate and mix well.

Heat the cream and date molasses in a saucepan over
medium heat until hot. Add to the chocolate mixture
and stir well, then cool to 50°C (122°F).

When the chocolate mixture is at the right temperature, blitz in the butter with a stick mixer until smooth. Allow the ganache to cool and become firm enough to pipe.

Fill a piping (icing) bag with a 9 mm (⅓ inch) plain nozzle with the ganache. Pipe the ganache on the flat side of half the macaron shells. Press a piece of fresh date into the centre of the ganache on each macaron. Top with the remaining macaron shells. Put the assembled macarons in the refrigerator for 24 hours to set, then bring to room temperature and serve or transfer to an airtight container.

**NOTE:** You can replace the dates in the date purée with the same weight of dried figs or 250 g (9 oz) fresh ginger, peeled and chopped, for a change of flavour.

1 quantity macaron shells (see page 98), coloured light brown
13 fresh dates, stoned and quartered

# CHILDHOOD SWEETHEART

# GINGERBREAD HOUSE

## GINGERBREAD

125 g (4½ oz) unsalted
   butter, chopped and
   softened
78 g (2¾ oz) brown sugar
40 g (1½ oz) golden syrup
60 g (2¼ oz) lightly
   beaten egg
375 g (13 oz) plain
   (all-purpose) flour
6 g (⅕ oz) ground ginger
1.5 g (¹⁄₂₀ oz) bicarbonate
   of soda (baking soda)
1 g (¹⁄₂₅ oz) ground cloves

## ROYAL ICING

40 g (1½ oz) egg white
2 g (²⁄₂₅ oz) lemon juice
180 g (6¼ oz) pure icing
   (confectioners') sugar,
   sifted

## SPICE MIX

1 g (¹⁄₂₅ oz) ground cloves
1 g (¹⁄₂₅ oz) ground ginger
1 g (¹⁄₂₅ oz) ground cinnamon

*contd ››*

**MAKES 50**

To make the gingerbread, put the butter, sugar and golden syrup in an electric mixer with a beater attachment and beat until pale and creamy. Beat in the egg.

Add the sifted dry ingredients and beat until the dough comes together as a ball. Transfer to a lightly floured work surface and knead until smooth.

Flatten the dough to a disc, about 2 cm (¾ inch) thick, and wrap in plastic wrap. Refrigerate for about 2 hours, until firm.

Meanwhile, to make the royal icing, put the egg white and lemon juice in an electric mixer with a whisk attachment and whisk, slowly adding the icing sugar, until all the icing sugar is incorporated and the mixture is smooth. Transfer to a bowl and press a sheet of plastic wrap onto the surface, then refrigerate until required.

Preheat the oven to 200°C (400°F/Gas 6). Line a baking tray with non-stick baking paper.

Weigh out 50 g (1¾ oz) of dough. Use a lightly floured rolling pin to roll out the dough on a lightly floured surface to a thickness of 3 mm (¹⁄₁₀ inch). Transfer to the lined tray and bake for 10 minutes, until golden. Allow to cool on the tray, then blitz in a food processor to fine crumbs.

To make the spice mix, put all the spices in a small bowl and mix well.

To make the gingerbread buttercream, put the egg yolks, milk and sugar in a saucepan and lightly whisk until combined, then heat over medium to low heat, stirring often, until the mixture reaches 85°C (185°F) or coats the back of a spoon.

Transfer to an electric mixer with a whisk attachment and whisk until the mixture cools to 30°C (86°F). Slowly add the butter, whisking until it is all incorporated.

Fold through the 25 g (⁹⁄₁₀ oz) royal icing, 120 g (4¼ oz) Italian meringue and 36 g (1¼ oz) gingerbread crumbs, then fold through the spice mix.

Fill a piping (icing) bag with a 7 mm (³⁄₈ inch) plain nozzle with the gingerbread buttercream. Pipe the buttercream on the flat side of half the macaron shells, then top with the remaining shells. Put the assembled macarons in the refrigerator for 24 hours to set, then bring to room temperature and serve or transfer to an airtight container.

**NOTE:** You can pipe the macaron shells into the shape of gingerbread houses if you like. Draw a template and place it under the baking paper to guide you as you pipe. You can decorate them with lollies before baking, then with icing (frosting) once they are cooked and cooled.

The remaining gingerbread dough can be used to make gingerbread biscuits, decorated with royal icing and lollies.

## GINGERBREAD BUTTERCREAM

40 g (1½ oz) egg yolks

70 g (2½ oz) milk

60 g (2¼ oz) caster (superfine) sugar

250 g (9 oz) unsalted butter, chopped and softened

25 g (⁹⁄₁₀ oz) royal icing (see recipe opposite)

120 g (4¼ oz) Italian meringue (see page 102)

36 g (1¼ oz) gingerbread crumbs (see recipe opposite)

1 quantity macaron shells, coloured brown (see Note)

# CHOCOLATE MARSHMALLOW LOLLIPOP

130 g (4½ oz) caster
  (superfine) sugar
221 g (7¾ oz) water
60 g (2¼ oz) liquid glucose
165 g (5¾ oz) inverted sugar
  (see Glossary)
18 g (⅔ oz) gold gelatine
  leaves (see Glossary)
61 g (2¼ oz) cocoa mass
  (see Glossary)
25 g (⁹⁄₁₀ oz) cocoa butter
  (see Glossary),
  finely chopped
50 lollipop sticks (see Note)
500 g (1 lb 2 oz) dark
  couverture chocolate
  (64%), tempered
  (see pages 106–107)
Roughly chopped roasted
  unsalted peanuts,
  for rolling

1 quantity chocolate
  macaron shells
  (see page 98)

**MAKES 50**

Put the caster sugar, 113 g (4 oz) of the water, the glucose and 80 g (2¾ oz) of the inverted sugar in a saucepan over medium heat and cook, without stirring, until the mixture reaches 113°C (235°F). Meanwhile, cut the gelatine into 2 cm (¾ inch) squares, put in a bowl with the remaining 108 g (3¾ oz) of water and set aside to soak.

Put the cocoa mass in a heatproof bowl over a saucepan of simmering water (make sure the base of the bowl doesn't touch the water) and stir until melted.

Put the remaining 85 g (3 oz) of inverted sugar in an electric mixer with a whisk attachment. When the sugar syrup is at the right temperature, turn on the mixer and pour it in a thin, steady stream over the inverted sugar, then whisk for 1 minute. Add the gelatine and soaking water and whisk until cooled.

Melt the cocoa butter in a small saucepan over low heat, then cool to 32°C (90°F). When the cocoa butter is at the right temperature, whisk it into the sugar mixture along with the melted cocoa mass. Set aside for a few minutes, until the marshmallow is firm enough to pipe.

Fill a piping (icing) bag with a 7 mm (⅜ inch) plain nozzle with the marshmallow. Pipe the marshmallow on the flat side of half the macaron shells, then press one end of a lollipop stick into the marshmallow on each and top with the remaining shells. Set aside for 1–2 hours for the marshmallow to firm and set.

Dip each macaron in the tempered chocolate, tap off the excess and then roll in the peanuts. Place the macarons on a baking tray lined with non-stick baking paper and refrigerate until set. Bring to room temperature and serve or transfer to an airtight container.

**NOTE:** Lollipop sticks are available from cake decorating suppliers, some supermarkets and lolly (candy) shops.

# STRAWBERRY BUBBLEGUM

150 g (5½ oz) strawberry purée (see page 105)

4 pieces (30 g/1 oz) original flavour Hubba Bubba® bubblegum, chopped

250 g (9 oz) white couverture chocolate, chopped or buttons

80 g (2¾ oz) unsalted butter, chopped and softened

25 g (⁹⁄₁₀ oz) cocoa butter (see Glossary), finely chopped, melted and cooled to 32°C (90°F)

## POPROCK INSERT

20 g (¾ oz) cocoa butter, finely chopped, melted and cooled to 32°C (90°F)

50 g (1¾ oz) plain poprocks (see Glossary)

1 quantity macaron shells (see page 98), coloured pink

**MAKES 50**

Put the strawberry purée and bubblegum in a saucepan over medium heat and cook until the bubblegum softens, then blitz with a stick mixer until smooth.

Put the chocolate in a bowl. Pour over the hot bubblegum mixture and set aside for 2 minutes. Stir until smooth, then cool the mixture to 50°C (122°F).

When the chocolate mixture is at the right temperature, blitz in the butter and 32°C (90°F) cocoa butter with a stick mixer until smooth. Allow the ganache to cool and become firm enough to pipe.

Meanwhile, to make the poprock insert, combine the 32°C (90°F) cocoa butter and poprocks in a small bowl. Roll the mixture out between two sheets of non-stick baking paper to about 2–3 mm (¹⁄₁₆–¹⁄₁₀ inch) thick, then leave at room temperature to set.

Fill a piping (icing) bag with a 7 mm (⅜ inch) plain nozzle with the ganache. Pipe the ganache on the flat side of half the macaron shells. Break off a piece of the poprock insert and put it on the ganache. Pipe another small amount of ganache over the poprock insert and top with the remaining macaron shells. Put the assembled macarons in the refrigerator for 24 hours to set, then bring to room temperature and serve or transfer to an airtight container.

# EASTER EGG YOLK

**MAKES 50**

To make the passionfruit gel, put the passionfruit juice, water and vanilla seeds in a saucepan and bring to 60°C (140°F).

Put the sugar and pectin NH in a small bowl and mix well. Whisk into the passionfruit mixture, then bring to the boil. Stir in the citric acid solution. Remove from the heat, pour into a heatproof bowl and set aside to cool completely.

To make the almond milk ganache, preheat the oven to 180°C (350°F/Gas 4). Roast the diced almonds until light golden, about 12 minutes, then set aside to cool.

Put the almond milk and vanilla seeds in a saucepan over medium heat and bring to the boil. Put the chocolate in a bowl. Pour over the hot milk and set aside for 2 minutes. Stir until smooth, then bring the mixture to 50°C (122°F).

When the chocolate mixture is at the right temperature, blitz in the butter with a stick mixer until smooth. Stir through the roasted almonds. Allow the ganache to cool and become firm enough to pipe.

Fill a piping (icing) bag with a 7 mm (³⁄₈ inch) plain nozzle with the ganache and another piping bag with the same size nozzle with the passionfruit gel. Pipe the ganache on the flat side of half the macaron shells, then pipe the passionfruit gel into the centre of the ganache. Top with the remaining shells. Put the assembled macarons in the refrigerator for 24 hours to set, then bring to room temperature and serve or transfer to an airtight container.

**NOTE:** If you would like to encase the passionfruit gel in chocolate (as pictured on page 53), see page 103.

## PASSIONFRUIT GEL

200 g (7 oz) fresh
    passionfruit juice
    (see Note, page 6)
100 g (3½ oz) water
Seeds scraped from
    1 vanilla bean
25 g (⁹⁄₁₀ oz) caster
    (superfine) sugar
4 g (³⁄₂₀ oz) pectin NH
    (see Glossary)
4 g (³⁄₂₀ oz) citric acid
    solution (see page 105)

## ALMOND MILK GANACHE

60 g (2¼ oz) diced almonds
150 g (5½ oz) almond milk
    (see Glossary)
Seeds scraped from
    1 vanilla bean
300 g (10½ oz) white
    couverture chocolate,
    chopped or buttons
25 g (⁹⁄₁₀ oz) unsalted butter,
    chopped and softened

1 quantity macaron shells
    (see page 98)

# FINGERBUN

150 g (5½ oz) thin (pouring/
  whipping) cream (35% fat)
2 g (²/₂₅ oz) ground cinnamon
250 g (9 oz) white couverture
  chocolate, chopped
  or buttons
100 g (3½ oz) raisins,
  roughly chopped
50 g (1¾ oz) desiccated
  coconut, plus extra,
  for rolling
50 g (1¾ oz) croissant,
  finely chopped (see Note)

1 quantity macaron shells
  (see page 98), coloured pink

**MAKES 50**

Put the cream and cinnamon in a saucepan over medium heat and bring to the boil. Put the chocolate in a bowl. Pour over the hot cream mixture and set aside for 2 minutes. Stir until smooth, then fold through the raisins, coconut and croissant. Allow the ganache to cool and become firm enough to pipe.

Fill a piping (icing) bag with a 7 mm (⅜ inch) plain nozzle with the ganache. Pipe the ganache on the flat side of half the macaron shells, then top with the remaining shells, ensuring the ganache comes right to the edge of each shell. Roll the macarons in the extra coconut. Put the assembled macarons in the refrigerator for 24 hours to set, then bring to room temperature and serve or transfer to an airtight container.

**NOTE:** Use a food processor to finely chop the croissant.

# SALTED BUTTER POPCORN

**MAKES 50**

Heat the sugar and water in a saucepan over medium–low heat until the sugar has dissolved. Increase the heat to medium and cook, without stirring, until the syrup reaches 121°C (250°F).

Put the egg and egg yolks in an electric mixer with a whisk attachment and whisk on medium speed for 2 minutes. When the syrup is at the right temperature, turn on the mixer and pour it in a thin steady stream over the egg. Continue to whisk until thick and cooled to 50°C (122°F). (Stop the mixer when checking the temperature.)

Slowly add the butter, a cube at a time, mixing well to ensure there are no lumps. Fold through the salt.

Fill a piping (icing) bag with a 7 mm (⅜ inch) plain nozzle with buttercream. Pipe the buttercream on the flat side of half the macaron shells, then top with the remaining shells.

Cook the popcorn according to the instructions on the bag. Put half the popcorn in a food processor and blitz to small pieces. (You can eat the popcorn remaining in the bag as it won't be needed.) Lightly brush the tops of the macarons with melted butter and sprinkle with the blitzed popcorn. Leave for 10 minutes so the butter can set.

Put the assembled macarons in the refrigerator for 24 hours to set, then bring to room temperature and serve or transfer to an airtight container.

**NOTE:** If you are using natural popcorn, you will need to add salt and butter after cooking it in the microwave.

## BUTTERCREAM

100 g (3½ oz) caster (superfine) sugar
38 g (1⅓ oz) water
75 g (2¾ oz) lightly beaten egg
45 g (1¾ oz) egg yolks
200 g (7 oz) unsalted butter, chopped and softened
3 g (¹⁄₁₀ oz) sea salt flakes

1 bag microwave natural or butter-flavoured popcorn (see Note)
Melted unsalted butter, for brushing

1 quantity macaron shells (see page 98), coloured white by mixing a little white food colouring powder with a tiny bit of water and adding to the sugar syrup

# CANDY CANE

200 g (7 oz) thin (pouring/ whipping) cream (35% fat)
70 g (2½ oz) candy canes, crushed
300 g (10½ oz) white couverture chocolate, chopped or buttons
60 g (2¼ oz) unsalted butter, chopped and softened

1 quantity macaron shells (see page 98), half coloured red and half coloured white by mixing a little white food colouring powder with a tiny bit of water and adding to the sugar syrup. Lay the piping bag on the table and spoon in the white mixture, then pick it up and spoon in the red mixture. Pipe in the shape of a candy cane — the colours will swirl together as you pipe (see Note)

**MAKES 50**

Put the cream and crushed candy canes in a saucepan over medium heat and bring to the boil, making sure the candies dissolve completely. Put the chocolate in a bowl. Pour over the hot cream mixture and set aside for 2 minutes. Stir until smooth, then cool the mixture to 50°C (122°F).

When the chocolate mixture is at the right temperature, blitz in the butter with a stick mixer until smooth. Allow the ganache to cool and become firm enough to pipe.

Fill a piping (icing) bag with a 7 mm (⅜ inch) plain nozzle with the ganache. Pipe the ganache on the flat side of half the macaron shells, then top with the remaining shells. Put the assembled macarons in the refrigerator for 24 hours to set, then bring to room temperature and serve or transfer to an airtight container.

**NOTE:** You might like to draw a template and place it under the baking paper to guide you as you pipe.

# TOASTED MARSHMALLOW

**MAKES 50**

Put the marshmallows on a baking tray and use a kitchen blowtorch to toast them on all sides.

Put the butter in an electric mixer with a paddle attachment. Cream the butter until it is pale. Add the 100 g (3½ oz) crème pâtissière and mix until well combined. Add the freshly toasted marshmallows and mix well.

Fill a piping (icing) bag with a 7 mm (⅜ inch) plain nozzle with the marshmallow mixture. Pipe the marshmallow mixture on the flat side of half the macaron shells, then top with the remaining shells. Put the assembled macarons in the refrigerator for 24 hours to set, then bring to room temperature and serve or transfer to an airtight container.

150 g (5½ oz) marshmallows
170 g (5¾ oz) unsalted butter, chopped and softened
100 g (3½ oz) crème pâtissière (see page 104)

1 quantity macaron shells (see page 98), half coloured pale pink, half coloured white by mixing a little white food colouring powder with a tiny bit of water and adding to the sugar syrup

# COCKTAIL HOUR

## TONIC & CUCUMBER CUSTRIANO

30 g (1 oz) caster
(superfine) sugar
3.25 g (1/10 oz) iota
(see Glossary)
1.5 g (1/20 oz) kappa
(see Glossary)
195 g (7 oz) thin (pouring/
whipping) cream (35% fat)
150 g (5½ oz) cucumber,
puréed
150 g (5½ oz) tonic water
10 g (¼ oz) juniper berries

## SUGAR SYRUP

10 g (¼ oz) caster
(superfine) sugar
10 g (¼ oz) water

## GIN GEL

100 g (3½ oz) gin
10 g (¼ oz) sugar syrup
(see recipe above)
1.6 g (1/20) xanthan gum
(see Glossary)

*contd ››*

**MAKES 50**

To make the tonic & cucumber custriano, put the sugar, iota and kappa in a small bowl and mix well. Put the cream, cucumber purée, tonic water and juniper berries in a saucepan. Add the sugar mixture and blitz with a stick mixer until smooth. Bring the mixture to the boil over medium–high heat and boil for 1 minute.

Transfer the custriano to a bowl and press a sheet of plastic wrap onto the surface, then refrigerate overnight.

To make the sugar syrup, put the sugar and water in a saucepan and bring to the boil, then remove from the heat and cool slightly.

To make the gin gel, put the gin, 10 g (¼ oz) of the sugar syrup and the xanthan gum in a saucepan and blitz with a stick mixer until smooth. Put over medium heat and bring to 60°C (140°F), then remove from the heat and set aside to cool to room temperature.

To make the tonic & cucumber custriano filling, put 250 g (9 oz) of the custriano in an electric mixer with a whisk attachment. Whisk on medium speed, slowly adding the butter until it is all incorporated.

Fill a piping (icing) bag with a 7 mm (⅜ inch) plain nozzle with the tonic & cucumber custriano filling and another piping bag with the same size nozzle with the gin gel.

Pipe the custriano filling on the flat side of half the macaron shells. Pipe a small amount of the gin gel into the custriano filling, ensuring it is covered by custriano (it may be necessary to pipe another small amount of custriano on top of the gel). Top with the remaining shells. Put the assembled macarons in the refrigerator for 24 hours to set, then bring to room temperature and serve or transfer to an airtight container.

### TONIC & CUCUMBER CUSTRIANO FILLING

250 g (9 oz) tonic and cucumber custriano (see recipe opposite)
100 g (3½ oz) unsalted butter, chopped, at room temperature

1 quantity macaron shells (see page 98), coloured green

# WASABI & PICKLED GINGER

9 g (¼ oz) wasabi powder
(see Glossary)
9 g (¼ oz) water
180 g (6¼ oz) thin (pouring/
whipping) cream (35% fat)
270 g (9½ oz) white
couverture chocolate,
chopped or buttons
60 g (2¼ oz) unsalted butter,
chopped and softened
12 g (⅖ oz) pickled ginger,
finely chopped

1 quantity macaron shells
(see page 98), coloured
black and sprinkled with
wasabi sesame seeds
(see Note and Glossary)

**MAKES 50**

Combine the wasabi powder and water to form a paste.
Put the cream in a saucepan and whisk in the wasabi paste
until smooth. Bring to the boil over medium heat. Put the
chocolate in a bowl. Pour over the hot cream mixture and
set aside for 2 minutes. Stir until smooth, then gently heat
to 50°C (122°F).

When the chocolate mixture is at the right temperature,
blitz in the butter with a stick mixer until smooth. Fold
through the ginger. Allow the ganache to cool and become
firm enough to pipe.

Fill a piping (icing) bag with a 7 mm (⅜ inch) plain nozzle
with the ganache. Pipe the ganache on the flat side of half
the macaron shells, then top with the remaining shells.
Put the assembled macarons in the refrigerator for 24 hours
to set, then bring to room temperature and serve or transfer
to an airtight container.

**NOTE:** If you can't get wasabi sesame seeds, shake regular
sesame seeds with green food colouring in a snap-lock bag.

# SALT & VINEGAR

**MAKES 50**

Put the cream in a saucepan over medium heat and bring to the boil. Put the chocolate in a bowl. Pour over the hot cream and set aside for 2 minutes. Stir until the mixture is smooth, then stir in the vinegar. Fold through the sea salt. Allow the ganache to cool and become firm enough to pipe.

Fill a piping (icing) bag with a 7 mm (⅜ inch) plain nozzle with the ganache. Pipe the ganache on the flat side of half the macaron shells, then top with the remaining shells. Put the assembled macarons in the refrigerator for 24 hours to set, then bring to room temperature and serve or transfer to an airtight container.

150 g (5½ oz) thin (pouring/whipping) cream (35% fat)

250 g (9 oz) white couverture chocolate, chopped or buttons

60 g (2¼ oz) balsamic vinegar

2 g (²⁄₂₅ oz) sea salt flakes

1 quantity macaron shells (see page 98), coloured with a little pink and a little purple food colouring

# EUCALYPTUS

**MAKES 50**

226 g (8 oz) thin (pouring/
   whipping) cream (35% fat)
96 g (3⅓ oz) eucalyptus
   drops (lollies), crushed
260 g (9¼ oz) white
   couverture chocolate,
   chopped or buttons
1 drop eucalyptus oil
   (see Glossary)
70 g (2½ oz) unsalted butter,
   chopped and softened

1 quantity macaron
   shells (see page 98),
   coloured green

Put the cream and crushed eucalyptus drops in a saucepan over medium–high heat and bring to the boil, making sure all the lollies have dissolved. Put the chocolate in a bowl. Pour over the hot cream and set aside for 2 minutes. Stir until smooth, then stir in the eucalyptus oil. Cool the mixture to 50°C (122°F).

When the chocolate mixture is at the right temperature, blitz in the butter with a stick mixer until smooth. Allow the ganache to cool and become firm enough to pipe.

Fill a piping (icing) bag with a 7 mm (⅜ inch) plain nozzle with the ganache. Pipe the ganache on the flat side of half the macaron shells, then top with the remaining shells. Put the assembled macarons in the refrigerator for 24 hours to set, then bring to room temperature and serve or transfer to an airtight container.

# COLA

**MAKES 50**

To make the cola custriano, put the cream, cola flavours, iota and kappa in a saucepan and blitz with a stick mixer to ensure the iota and kappa are thoroughly incorporated. Bring to the boil over medium heat. Boil for 1 minute, then remove from the heat. Transfer to a bowl and press a sheet of plastic wrap onto the surface. Refrigerate overnight.

To make the fizzy dust, put the citric acid and bicarbonate of soda in a small bowl and mix well.

To make the cola custriano filling, put 250 g (9 oz) of the cola custriano in an electric mixer with a whisk attachment. Whisk on medium speed, slowly adding the butter until it is all incorporated.

Fill a piping (icing) bag with a 7 mm (⅜ inch) plain nozzle with the cola custriano filling. Pipe the filling on the flat side of half the macaron shells, sprinkle with fizzy dust, then top with the remaining shells. Sprinkle the shells with more fizzy dust. Put the assembled macarons in the refrigerator for 24 hours to set, then bring to room temperature and serve or transfer to an airtight container.

## COLA CUSTRIANO

130 g (4½ oz) thin (pouring/whipping) cream (35% fat)

35 g (1¼ oz) sugar-free cola flavour (Sodastream™) (see Glossary)

15 g (½ oz) cola flavour (Sodastream™) (see Glossary)

1.5 g (¹⁄₂₀ oz) iota (see Glossary)

0.5 g (¹⁄₅₀ oz) kappa (see Glossary)

## FIZZY DUST

25 g (⁹⁄₁₀ oz) citric acid (see Glossary)

25 g (⁹⁄₁₀ oz) bicarbonate of soda (baking soda)

## COLA CUSTRIANO FILLING

250 g (9 oz) cola custriano (see recipe above)

50 g (1¾ oz) unsalted butter, chopped, at room temperature

1 quantity macaron shells (see page 98), coloured red

# SATAY

## SATAY SAUCE

5 g (1/8 oz) vegetable oil

2 g (2/25 oz) finely
  chopped garlic

4 g (3/20 oz) ground turmeric

2.5 g (2/25 oz) ground chilli

60 g (2¼ oz) coconut milk

60 g (2¼ oz) smooth
  peanut butter

8 g (¼ oz) palm sugar
  (jaggery), grated

4 g (3/20 oz) soy sauce

*contd ››*

**MAKES 50**

To make the satay sauce, heat the oil in a frying pan over medium–low heat and cook the garlic until softened. Add the turmeric and cook until aromatic, then add the chilli and cook for 1 minute. Add the coconut milk, peanut butter, palm sugar and soy sauce and bring to the boil. Remove from the heat.

To make the satay ganache, put 115 g (4 oz) of the satay sauce and the cream in a saucepan over medium heat and bring to the boil. Put the chocolate in a bowl. Pour over the hot cream mixture and set aside for 2 minutes. Stir until smooth, then cool the mixture to 50°C (122°F).

When the chocolate mixture is at the right temperature, blitz in the butter with a stick mixer until smooth. Fold through the peanuts. Allow the ganache to cool and become firm enough to pipe.

Fill a piping (icing) bag with a 7 mm (⅜ inch) plain nozzle with the ganache. Pipe the ganache on the flat side of half the macaron shells, then top with the remaining shells. Put the assembled macarons in the refrigerator for 24 hours to set, then bring to room temperature and serve or transfer to an airtight container.

**NOTE:** To make the red flecks, dip a pastry brush in red food colouring and flick over the macaron shells.

### SATAY GANACHE

115 g (4 oz) satay sauce
  (see recipe opposite)
130 g (4½ oz) thin (pouring/
  whipping) cream (35% fat)
215 g (7½ oz) white
  couverture chocolate,
  chopped or buttons
70 g (2½ oz) unsalted butter,
  chopped and softened
60 g (2¼ oz) finely chopped
  roasted unsalted peanuts

1 quantity macaron shells
  (see page 98), coloured
  light orange with flecks
  of red (see Note)

# PISTACHIO

75 g (2¾ oz) thin (pouring/
   whipping) cream (35% fat)
22 g (¾ oz) inverted sugar
   (see Glossary)
1 g (¹⁄₂₅ oz) ground
   cardamom
350 g (12 oz) white
   couverture chocolate,
   chopped or buttons
65 g (2⅓ oz) toasted
   pistachio paste
   (see page 104)
22 g (¾ oz) untoasted
   pistachio paste
   (see page 104)
37 g (1⅓ oz) unsalted butter,
   chopped and softened
2 g (²⁄₂₅ oz) sea salt flakes

1 quantity macaron shells
   (see page 98), coloured
   light green

**MAKES 50**

Put the cream, sugar and cardamom in a saucepan over medium heat and bring to the boil. Put the chocolate in a bowl. Pour over the hot cream mixture and set aside for 2 minutes. Stir until smooth, then cool the mixture to 50°C (122°F).

When the chocolate mixture is at the right temperature, blitz in the pistachio pastes and butter with a stick mixer until smooth. Stir through the sea salt. Allow the ganache to cool and become firm enough to pipe.

Fill a piping (icing) bag with a 7 mm (⅜ inch) plain nozzle with the ganache. Pipe the ganache on the flat side of half the macaron shells, then top with the remaining shells. Put the assembled macarons in the refrigerator for 24 hours to set, then bring to room temperature and serve or transfer to an airtight container.

# FIG, BURNT HONEY & RED WINE

**MAKES 50**

250 g (9 oz) dried figs, roughly chopped
50 g (1¾ oz) honey
56 g (2 oz) kumabo couverture chocolate (80%) (see Glossary), chopped or buttons
63 g (2⅓ oz) red wine
63 g (2⅓ oz) unsalted butter, chopped and softened

1 quantity macaron shells (see page 98), coloured bright green

Put the figs in a heatproof bowl, then pour over enough boiling water to cover. Set aside for about 1 hour, until the figs are rehydrated. Drain the excess liquid. Purée the soaked figs in a food processor until smooth.

Put the honey in a saucepan over medium heat and cook for 3–4 minutes, until the colour deepens and it just begins to burn.

Put the chocolate in a large heatproof bowl over a saucepan of simmering water (make sure the base of the bowl doesn't touch the water) and stir until melted. Add the fig purée, burnt honey and red wine and mix well, then gently heat to 50°C (122°F).

When the chocolate mixture is at the right temperature, blitz in the butter with a stick mixer until smooth. Allow the ganache to cool and become firm enough to pipe.

Fill a piping (icing) bag with a 7 mm (⅜ inch) plain nozzle with the ganache. Pipe the ganache on the flat side of half the macaron shells, then top with the remaining shells. Put the assembled macarons in the refrigerator for 24 hours to set, then bring to room temperature and serve or transfer to an airtight container.

# KALAMATA OLIVE

## CANDIED KALAMATA OLIVE PURÉE

225 g (8 oz) kalamata olives, pitted
375 g (13 oz) caster (superfine) sugar
750 g (1 lb 10 oz) water

## LEMON CANDIES

195 g (6⁴/₅ oz) isomalt (see Glossary)
Finely grated zest of ⅓ lemon
18 g (²/₃ oz) earl grey tea (see Note)
4.5 g (⅛ oz) bergamot essential oil (see Glossary)

*contd ››*

**MAKES 50**

To make the candied kalamata olive purée, fill a medium saucepan three-quarters full of water and bring to the boil. Put the olives in a sieve and rinse them under cool running water. Add to the boiling water, return to the boil and then drain the olives immediately, rinse and drain again. Repeat this process five times.

Heat the sugar and water in a saucepan over low heat until the sugar has dissolved, then increase the heat to medium and bring the sugar syrup to the boil. Add the olives and boil for 20 minutes. Remove from the heat and cool the olives in the syrup.

Drain 150 g (5½ oz) of the candied olives, put in a food processor and blend until smooth.

To make the lemon candies, lightly spray a baking tray with cooking oil and line with non-stick baking paper. Put the tray in the freezer.

Put the isomalt, lemon zest and tea in a heavy-based saucepan and stir occasionally over medium heat until the isomalt has dissolved. Continue cooking until the mixture reaches 170°C (338°F), then add the bergamot.

Using a heated teaspoon, drop a spoonful (about 2 cm/ ¾ inch diameter) of hot isomalt mixture onto the cold tray. Reheat the teaspoon and repeat until all the mixture is used. Allow the candies to cool and harden.

To make the kalamata olive ganache, melt the chocolate in a heatproof bowl over a saucepan of simmering water

(make sure the base of the bowl doesn't touch the water) or in the microwave on medium (50%) in 30-second bursts, stirring after each burst. Take care not to burn the chocolate as it will become grainy.

Put 150 g (5½ oz) of the candied kalamata olive purée in an electric mixer with a whisk attachment. With the motor running on low speed, pour the melted chocolate over the olive purée and whisk for 1 minute.

Slowly add the butter, a cube at a time, continuing to whisk until all the butter has been added and the mixture is smooth. Slowly add the olive oil in a thin steady stream, whisking until the mixture is homogeneous. Remove the bowl from the mixer and use a spatula or spoon to fold through the chopped olives. Allow the ganache to cool and become firm enough to pipe.

Fill a piping (icing) bag with a 12 mm (½ inch) plain nozzle with the ganache. Pipe the ganache on the flat side of half the macaron shells. Press a lemon candy into the centre of the ganache on each macaron. Top with the remaining shells. Put the assembled macarons in the refrigerator for 24 hours to set, then bring to room temperature and serve or transfer to an airtight container.

**NOTE:** Make a strong infusion of earl grey tea, then strain and measure out 18 g (⅔ oz) of liquid.

### KALAMATA OLIVE GANACHE

300 g (10½ oz) white couverture chocolate, chopped or buttons

150 g (5½ oz) candied kalamata olive purée (see recipe opposite)

48 g (1¾ oz) unsalted butter, chopped and softened

48 g (1¾ oz) extra virgin olive oil

48 g (1¾ oz) kalamata olives, pitted and finely chopped

1 quantity macaron shells (see page 98), coloured dark purple

# ZUMBARON DESSERTS

# RASPBERRY SHORTBREAD ZUMBARON TARTS

*You can use any zumbarons in these tarts, even those that are damaged or soggy. If they have a softer filling, such as a buttercream, or jelly-based insert, add them after baking and cooling the tarts.*

## PÂTE SUCRÉE

125 g (4½ oz) unsalted butter, chopped and softened

85 g (3 oz) pure icing (confectioners') sugar, sifted

Seeds scraped from 1 vanilla bean

60 g (2¼ oz) egg

210 g (7½ oz) plain (all-purpose) flour, sifted

## ALMOND CREAM

190 g (6¾ oz) unsalted butter, chopped and softened

220 g (7¾ oz) caster (superfine) sugar

*contd ››*

**MAKES 6**

To make the pâte sucrée, put the butter, icing sugar and vanilla seeds in an electric mixer with a beater attachment. Beat on low speed for 2–3 minutes, until combined. Increase the speed to medium and beat for a further 2–3 minutes to slightly aerate the mixture. Add the egg and beat until combined. Scrape down the bowl, then add the flour and mix until just combined.

Place a sheet of plastic wrap on your work surface. Spoon the soft dough onto the plastic, then fold the plastic over it and press down to a disc, about 2 cm (¾ inch) thick. Refrigerate for about 2 hours, until firm.

To make the almond cream, put the butter and sugar in an electric mixer with a beater attachment and beat until combined. With the motor running, slowly add the beaten egg and egg yolks until combined. Fold through the almond meal, crème pâtissière and vanilla. Transfer to a container, cover with plastic wrap and refrigerate.

To make the raspberry gel, heat the purée in a medium saucepan until it reaches 60°C (140°F). Put the sugar and pectin NH in a small bowl and mix well. When the purée is at the right temperature, sprinkle over the sugar mixture and whisk until combined. Bring the mixture to the boil. Add the citric acid solution, then remove from the heat. Pour into a bowl, cover with plastic wrap and set aside to cool.

Preheat the oven to 200°C (400°F/Gas 6).

To assemble, lightly dust a work surface with flour and use a lightly floured rolling pin to roll out the pâte sucrée dough to a 3 mm (1/10 inch) thickness. Use a round 10 cm (4 inch) cutter to cut out 6 discs and ease each disc into an 8 cm (3¼ inch) loose-based tart (flan) tin. Put the tins on a baking tray, then cover each pastry shell with non-stick baking paper and fill with baking weights. Bake for about 10 minutes, until light golden. Remove from the oven, then carefully remove the baking weights and paper and set aside to cool completely. (You can use any leftover dough to make more tart shells and fill them however you like.)

Reduce the oven temperature to 190°C (375°F/Gas 5).

Pipe an 8 mm (3/8 inch) layer of raspberry gel into the bottom of each tart shell. Put 3 fresh raspberries on top of the gel. Use a teaspoon to fill the tart shells with the almond cream, then smooth it out until it is flush with the top of each tart shell.

Bake the tarts for 10–15 minutes, until the almond cream is puffed and light golden. Remove from the oven and arrange 3 raspberry shortbread zumbarons, slightly overlapping, on top of each tart. Return to the oven for 5 minutes more. Transfer to a wire rack to cool completely.

Remove the cooled tarts from their tins. Scatter 4 fresh raspberries on top of each. Dust the icing sugar over the flaked almonds, then place the almonds on the tarts.

**NOTE:** Don't worry if the almond cream splits when adding the eggs and yolks — it will come back together when you add the almond meal. If it bothers you, you can heat the bowl slightly with a kitchen blowtorch to bring it back together immediately.

160 g (5½ oz) lightly beaten egg
50 g (1¾ oz) egg yolks
220 g (7¾ oz) almond meal
100 g (3½ oz) crème pâtissière (see page 104)
5 g (1/8 oz) natural vanilla extract

### RASPBERRY GEL

500 g (1 lb 2 oz) raspberry purée (see page 105)
50 g (1¾ oz) caster (superfine) sugar
10 g (¼ oz) pectin NH (see Glossary)
8 g (¼ oz) citric acid solution (see page 105)

42 fresh raspberries
18 raspberry shortbread zumbarons (see page 38)
Pure icing (confectioners') sugar, for dusting
Toasted flaked almonds, to decorate

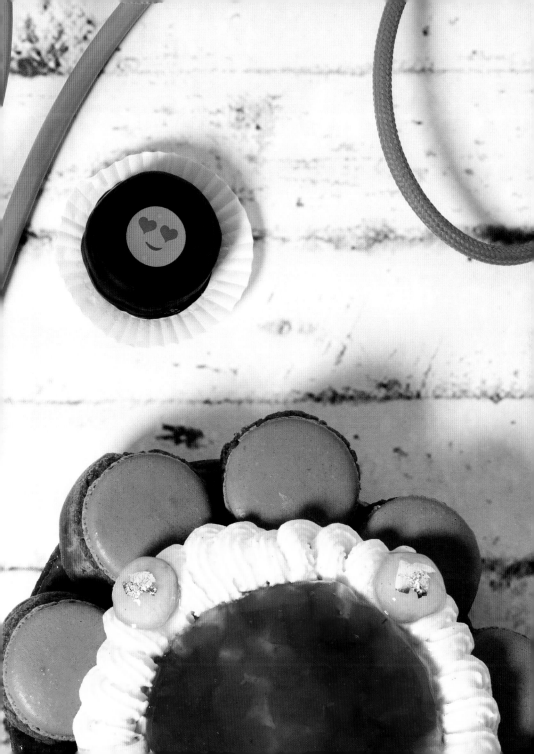

# ST CHOUXMACA

*This blissful dessert combines choux puffs, crisp sablé, caramelised apple, crème chantilly and macarons.*

## VANILLA CRÈME CHANTILLY

4 g (³/₂₀ oz) gold gelatine leaves (see Glossary)
24 g (⁹/₁₀ oz) cold water
590 g (1 lb 4¾ oz) thin (pouring/whipping) cream (35% fat)
175 g (6 oz) caster (superfine) sugar
Seeds scraped from 2 vanilla beans

## CRÈME PÂTISSIÈRE CARAMEL

250 g (9 oz) caster (superfine) sugar
250 g (9 oz) water
1 kg (2 lb 4 oz) milk
250 g (9 oz) egg yolks
250 g (9 oz) caster (superfine) sugar
100 g (3½ oz) cornflour (cornstarch)
100 g (3½ oz) unsalted butter, chopped and softened slightly
2 g (²/₂₅ oz) sea salt flakes

*contd ››*

**SERVES 12**

To make the vanilla crème chantilly, cut the gelatine leaves into small squares, place in a bowl with the cold water and set aside until softened.

Meanwhile, put the cream, sugar and vanilla seeds in a saucepan over medium heat and bring to the boil. Remove from the heat and cool to 70–80°C (158–176°F). Add the gelatine and any soaking liquid and mix to combine. Place in a container and cool to room temperature, then cover with plastic wrap and press it onto the surface to prevent a skin forming. Refrigerate overnight.

To make the crème pâtissière caramel, put the sugar in a saucepan over medium–high heat. Cook until the sugar caramelises and reaches a dark-amber colour. Being careful not to burn yourself, add the water to deglaze the caramel. Stir until smooth and the caramel has dissolved. Set aside to cool. Bring the milk to the boil in a medium saucepan over medium heat. Remove from the heat. Use a balloon whisk to whisk the egg yolks, caster sugar and cornflour in a bowl until thick and pale. Stir through 150 g (5½ oz) of the cooled caramel (reserve the rest for another use).

Gradually whisk in one-quarter of the hot milk to bring the egg mixture to temperature. Add the mixture to the remaining milk and whisk constantly over medium heat until the custard comes to the boil and thickens. Transfer to a bowl and cover with plastic wrap, pressing it onto the surface to prevent a skin forming. Cool the crème pâtissière to 50°C (122°F), then use a balloon whisk to whisk in the butter and salt until smooth. Cover with plastic wrap as before and refrigerate to cool completely. Before using, use a balloon whisk to whisk until smooth.

To make the sablé à choux, put all the ingredients in an electric mixer with a beater attachment. Beat on low speed until the ingredients are just combined, then increase the speed to medium and beat for 2 minutes. Gather together into a ball, place on plastic wrap and pat down to a 2 cm (¾ inch) thick disc. Wrap up and refrigerate for 2 hours or until well chilled and firm.

Meanwhile, to make the apple tatin compôte, put the sugar in a saucepan over medium–high heat. Cook until the sugar dissolves and reaches a dark-amber colour. Being careful not to burn yourself, add the water to deglaze the caramel. Stir until smooth and the caramel has dissolved. Add the apples and cook until slightly translucent and tender. Remove from the heat and remove the apples from the liquid. Squeeze the water from the gelatine, then add to the liquid in the pan and stir to combine. Return to the heat and bring to the boil, then pour into a bowl and cool. Once cooled, whisk, then fold in the apples and salt.

Preheat the oven to 210°C (415°F/Gas 6–7). Lightly butter a large baking tray, then wipe off any excess with paper towels. Lightly flour a work surface and use a lightly floured rolling pin to roll the dough out to a thickness of 3 mm (¹⁄₁₀ inch). Use a round 6 cm (2½ inch) cutter to cut out 12 discs. Put on the greased tray, evenly spaced.

To make the choux pastry, put the milk, butter, water, sugar and salt in a heavy-based saucepan over medium heat and bring to the boil. Remove from the heat and quickly beat in the flour with a wooden spoon. Return the pan to the heat and continue beating until the mixture comes together and pulls away from the side of the pan. Beat over low heat for a further 1–2 minutes to cook the flour, then remove from the heat and allow the mixture to cool slightly.

Transfer to an electric mixer with a beater attachment and begin beating the mixture on medium speed to release some of the heat. Gradually add the egg, beating well after each addition, until all the egg has been added. Beat the mixture for several minutes more, until it is thick and glossy — a spoon should stand upright in it.

Working in batches, spoon some of the pastry mixture into a piping (icing) bag with a 12–15 mm (½–⅝ inch) plain

## SABLÉ À CHOUX
350 g (12 oz) plain (all-purpose) flour
300 g (10½ oz) brown sugar
300 g (10½ oz) chilled unsalted butter, cut into small dice

## APPLE TATIN COMPÔTE
500 g (1 lb 2 oz) caster (superfine) sugar
300 g (10½ oz) water
600 g (1 lb 5 oz) granny smith apples, peeled, cored, cut into 1 cm (½ inch) pieces
12.5 g (²⁄₅ oz) gold gelatine leaves, soaked in cold water until softened
5 g (⅛ oz) sea salt flakes

## CHOUX PASTRY
540 g (1 lb 3 oz) milk
400 g (14 oz) unsalted butter, chopped
430 g (15¼ oz) water
20 g (¾ oz) caster (superfine) sugar
20 g (¾ oz) fine salt
540 g (1 lb 3 oz) plain (all-purpose) flour, sifted
732 g (1 lb 9½ oz) lightly beaten eggs

contd ››

## TO ASSEMBLE

1 sheet frozen ready-made puff pastry, semi-thawed

40 g (1½ oz) caster (superfine) sugar

Pure icing (confectioners') sugar, to dust

12 macaron shells (see page 98), coloured green

100 g (3½ oz) clear neutral glaze (see page 102)

5 apple balls, cut with a melon baller and brushed with the clear neutral glaze

Gold leaf, to decorate

nozzle. Cover the remaining mixture with plastic wrap. Holding the nozzle about 2 cm (¾ inch) above the tray, in the centre of each sablé disc, slowly but firmly pipe the mixture without moving the bag from this position — the pastry will spread towards the edge of the disc. Stop piping just before it reaches the edge and move the nozzle from 12 o'clock to 6 o'clock quickly to finish the piping action. Bake for 25–30 minutes or until the choux is firm and sounds hollow when tapped. Set aside on the tray for 5 minutes, then transfer to a wire rack to cool completely.

Preheat the oven to 200°C (400°F/Gas 6). Using a round 22 cm (8½ inch) cake tin as a guide, cut a large disc from the pastry. Place on a baking tray lined with baking paper and prick all over with a fork. Sprinkle with sugar and bake for 8–10 minutes or until the pastry just starts to colour.

Remove the pastry from the oven. Press down on the pastry with another tray to squash out the air. Remove the tray and place a wire rack over the pastry to prevent it rising again. Reduce the oven temperature to 180°C (350°F/Gas 4) and bake for 15 minutes or until golden. Remove and take the rack away. Dust the pastry evenly with icing sugar. Increase the oven to 220°C (425°F/Gas 7) and bake for 7–8 minutes more, until the sugar caramelises (the caramel should be shiny like glass). Remove from the oven.

Cut a small hole in the top of each choux. Spoon the crème pâtissière caramel into a piping (icing) bag with a 7 mm (⅜ inch) plain nozzle. Half-fill each choux, then use a teaspoon to spoon over the apple tatin compote until full. Arrange around the edge of the pastry disc, sablé sides down. Top each with a macaron shell to cover the hole, using a little crème pâtissière caramel to stick them on.

Spoon the apple tatin compôte into the centre of the pastry disc so it is level with the tops of the chouxmacas. Carefully pour over enough clear neutral glaze to cover the surface. Whip the vanilla crème chantilly until firm. Spoon into a piping (icing) bag with a 7 mm (⅜ inch) star nozzle and pipe around the compôte. Arrange the apple balls on the chantilly and top each with gold leaf.

# CHOCARONS

**MAKES AS MANY AS YOU LIKE**

Place three-quarters of the chocolate in a medium heatproof bowl over a saucepan of simmering water (make sure the base of the bowl doesn't touch the water) and stir until melted. When the chocolate reaches 45–50°C (113–122°F) remove the bowl from the pan and continue to temper the chocolate using either the seeding or tabling method (see pages 106–107).

Place a sheet of non-stick baking paper next to the bowl of chocolate and have ready a dipping fork (or table fork) and a spatula.

Place one zumbaron at a time in the bowl of tempered chocolate. Use the fork to gently lift it out and agitate it slightly so the excess chocolate drips back into the bowl. Gently run the bottom of the fork over the edge of the bowl, then place the chocaron on the baking paper. Work from the far side to the closest side when placing the chocarons on the paper to avoid chocolate dripping over the finished chocarons.

Decorate the chocarons as you wish. Set aside for 2 hours for the chocolate to crystallise.

*Zumbarons that have been damaged or have gone soggy are the perfect contenders for dipping in dark, milk or white couverture chocolate. You can then decorate them or dust them with blitzed macaron shells to finish.*

Your choice of dark, milk
  or white couverture
  chocolate, chopped
  or buttons
Damaged or soggy
  zumbarons
Decorations or blitzed
  macaron dust, as desired

# ZUMBARON TOWER

Polystyrene cone
Zumbarons of choice
Double-ended toothpicks

Zumbarons with a firm filling, such as a ganache or buttercream, are best for this as those with soft fillings tend to sag and fall off the cone.

The number of zumbarons required depends on the size of your polystyrene cone. We use a cone that is 53 cm (21 inches) tall and 20 cm (8 inches) wide at the base, and this requires 120 zumbarons to cover it.

To assemble the zumbaron tower, insert toothpicks on a slight angle, tilting upwards, into the cone. Place the zumbarons on the toothpicks, creating a pattern as desired.

**NOTE:** It is important to use toothpicks to secure the zumbarons to the cone, rather than adhering them with something edible that sets hard, such as melted chocolate. Toothpicks retain the structure and presentation of the zumbarons, as the zumbarons can easily be lifted from the cone with nothing more than a small hole in them. If chocolate is used, you need to use force to remove the zumbarons from the cone and this will rip and break them.

# ZUMBARONI ROAD

**MAKES 25 PIECES**

Line the base and sides of a square 25 cm (10 inch) cake tin with non-stick baking paper, extending the paper 5 cm (2 inches) over the sides.

Place 1 kg (2 lb 4 oz) of the chocolate in a medium heatproof bowl over a saucepan of simmering water (make sure the base of the bowl doesn't touch the water) and stir until melted. When the chocolate reaches 45–50°C (113–122°F) remove the bowl from the pan and continue to temper the chocolate using either the seeding or tabling method (see pages 106–107).

Put all the remaining ingredients in a large bowl, then quickly stir through the chocolate until everything is well coated. Scrape the mixture into the prepared tin and tap the tin gently to allow the chocolate to settle. Set aside in a cool dry place for 2–3 hours to set.

Use the overhanging paper to lift the chocolate block out of the tin. Heat a large sharp knife by dipping it in hot water and then drying, and use it to cut the chocolate block into 5 cm (2 inch) squares.

**NOTE:** You will need 50–55 macaron shells to make up the required amount.

*One thing I love to do with imperfect or excess zumbarons is make my version of rocky road. You can change any component for something similar, such as using Turkish delight instead of marshmallows or chopped biscuits instead of rice cereal. If you have more or less of any ingredient (except for the chocolate), you can adjust the quantity of another ingredient to compensate, too.*

1.3 kg (3 lb) milk couverture chocolate, chopped or buttons
320 g (11¼ oz) macaron shells (see page 98, and Note)
100 g (3½ oz) toasted almonds
80 g (2¾ oz) desiccated coconut, toasted
80 g (2¾ oz) marshmallows
80 g (2¾ oz) plain puffed rice cereal
60 g (2¼ oz) glacé cherries

# ZUMBARON ICE CREAM SANDWICHES

1 quantity Italian meringue
  macarons mixture
  (see page 98)
200 g (7 oz) milk chocolate,
  chopped or buttons
200 g (7 oz) cocoa butter
  (see Glossary), chopped
50 g (1¾ oz) coarsely
  chopped toasted nuts

**VANILLA ICE CREAM**

1 kg (2 lb 4 oz) milk
300 g (10½ oz) thin
  (pouring/whipping) cream
  (35% fat)
2 vanilla beans, split
  lengthways and seeds
  scraped
235 g (8½ oz) caster
  (superfine) sugar
75 g (2¾ oz) full-cream
  milk powder
60 g (2¼ oz) egg yolks
20 g (¾ oz) liquid glucose

**MAKES 22**

To make the vanilla ice cream, put the milk and cream in a medium saucepan. Add the vanilla seeds and pods and bring to the boil. Remove from the heat and set aside for 1–2 hours to infuse (see Note).

Put the sugar, milk powder, egg yolks and glucose in a bowl and stir to combine.

Remove the vanilla beans from the milk. Reheat the milk until warm, then add one-quarter of the milk to the egg mixture to bring it to temperature. Add the egg mixture to the remaining milk in the pan and cook, stirring, over medium heat until the mixture reaches 85°C (185°F).

Fill a bowl with ice, then put another bowl inside it. Strain the mixture into the bowl over the ice. Leave to cool, stirring occasionally.

Once cooled, churn the mixture in an ice-cream machine according to the manufacturer's instructions.

Meanwhile, place a baking tray in the freezer.

Put a square 25 cm (10 inch) stainless-steel cake frame on the frozen tray. Use a spatula to turn the churned ice cream into the frame and spread it out evenly, being sure to remove any air pockets. Cover with plastic wrap and freeze overnight, until firm.

Fill a piping (icing) bag with a 7 mm (⅜ inch) plain nozzle with the Italian meringue macarons mixture. Pipe 8 cm (3¼ inch) diameter rounds (or rectangles, see Note) onto lined baking sheets, leaving enough room between each to allow for spreading and good air circulation so they cook evenly. Tap the trays lightly underneath to release excess air and flatten the macaron shells. Leave the macarons in a cool dry place for 30 minutes or until a skin forms. After 10 minutes, preheat the oven to 130°C (250°F/Gas 1).

To test if the macarons are ready, gently touch one with your fingertip to check that a light skin has formed — the macarons should not be sticky.

Place another baking sheet under each baking sheet holding macaron shells, then bake for about 16 minutes, until the macarons have a firm outer shell. Remove from the oven and slide the paper with the shells onto wire racks. Cool the macarons completely, then pair them up.

Put the chocolate and cocoa butter in a small saucepan over low heat until melted. Stir in the nuts and set aside.

Remove the ice cream from the freezer. Use hot water and a cloth to rub the frame until it releases the ice cream. Using a round 8 cm (3¼ inch) metal cutter dipped in hot water and then dried, cut the ice cream into rounds (or cut into rectangles). Sandwich each between a pair of macaron shells. Dip each sandwich halfway into the chocolate mixture, then transfer to a wire rack to set. Store in an airtight container in the freezer, layered with baking paper.

**NOTE:** You can infuse the milk the day before to give a more intense flavour if you like.

You can make rectangle 'sandwiches' if you prefer (as pictured on page 93). For the macarons, draw a rectangle on a piece of paper, then place it under the baking paper you are going to pipe on as a template. Alternatively, make a template out of plastic or silicone by cutting out the shape of a rectangle. Spread the mixture over the template using a palette knife and then lift away the template. Cut the ice cream into the same-sized rectangles.

BASICS

# ITALIAN MERINGUE MACARONS

*This is the best place to start your macaron ventures as it is the easiest and most trustworthy method, using an Italian meringue mixture with a high sugar content that guarantees a glossy shell. The zumbarons in this book were made using this reliable, all-purpose recipe.*

300 g (10½ oz) almond meal
300 g (10½ oz) pure icing (confectioners') sugar
110 g (3¾ oz) egg whites, at room temperature
300 g (10½ oz) caster (superfine) sugar
75 g (2¾ oz) water
Food colouring, if required (see Note)
2 g (2⁄25 oz) powdered egg white (see Glossary)
110 g (3¾ oz) egg whites, extra, at room temperature

**MAKES 100**

Grease 3 large baking sheets and line with non-stick baking paper or Silpat (see Glossary). Place another baking sheet under each lined baking sheet.

Put the almond meal and icing sugar in a food processor and process to a fine powder, then sift into a large bowl.

Put the egg whites in an electric mixer with a whisk attachment. Put the sugar and water in a small saucepan over low heat and stir until the sugar has dissolved. Use a clean pastry brush to brush down the side of the pan to avoid any crystallisation. Increase the heat and bring to the boil. Add the food colouring (if required) at this stage. Cook until the mixture reaches 118°C (244°F). When it is getting close to this temperature, add the powdered egg white to the egg whites in the mixing bowl and whisk on medium speed until frothy.

Once the sugar syrup is at the right temperature, add it to the egg whites in a thin steady stream down the side of the bowl. Whisk until warm, about 8 minutes. Add the extra egg whites to the dry ingredients, then add the meringue and use a large spatula to fold them through until combined.

Continue to fold the mixture so it begins to loosen. Working the mixture this way will soften it slightly — when the mixture falls slowly off the spatula it is at the right texture. The texture is important for the next stage, which is piping the macaron shells.

Transfer the mixture to a piping (icing) bag with a 7 mm (⅜ inch) plain nozzle. Holding the piping bag about 1.5 cm (⅝ inch) above a lined baking sheet, pipe straight down to make 4 cm (1½ inch) diameter rounds, leaving a 3 cm (1¼ inch) gap between each. As you finish piping each macaron, move the nozzle from 12 o'clock to 6 o'clock quickly to finish the piping action. If you have the correct texture, the macaron will soften again slightly and the tip on top of the macaron will drop, leaving a smooth top. Some macarons are dusted, using a fine sieve, or sprinkled with a flavour at this stage (refer to specific recipes).

Leave the macarons at room temperature for 30 minutes or until a skin forms. After 10 minutes, preheat the oven to 135°C (275°F/Gas 1).

To test if the macarons are ready, gently touch one with your fingertip to check that a light skin has formed — the macarons should not be sticky. On humid days this may take longer. The skin is important as it lifts while the macaron cooks, creating a 'foot' at the base.

Bake the macarons for 16 minutes, until they have a firm outer shell. Remove from the oven and set aside for 2 minutes, then carefully remove one macaron with a spatula to check that the base is also cooked and dry.

If it is still slightly sticky, return the macarons to the oven for 2–3 minutes, then check again. Cool the macarons completely on the trays, then pair them up according to size.

**NOTE:** Food colouring brands vary — some gels require only 2 or 3 drops to give the desired colour, while some liquids require far more. Getting the colour right comes down to practice — you need to see how the colour looks in the syrup and then how that changes when it combines with the other ingredients. If you need to colour the macarons with two colours, make two half-quantities, in separate batches, and add a different colour to each.

### VARIATION — CHOCOLATE MACARON SHELLS

Process 60 g (2¼ oz) unsweetened cocoa powder with 270 g (9½ oz) almond meal and 270 g (9½ oz) pure icing (confectioners') sugar, then sift and continue as for the basic recipe.

# SWISS MERINGUE MACARONS

An intermediate macaron recipe, the Swiss meringue has a higher degree of difficulty than the Italian meringue and less sugar.

300 g (10½ oz) almond meal
300 g (10½ oz) pure icing (confectioners') sugar
260 g (9¼ oz) egg whites, at room temperature
150 g (5½ oz) caster (superfine) sugar
4 g (³⁄₂₀ oz) powdered egg white (see Glossary)
Food colouring, if required

**MAKES 100**

Line 2 large baking sheets with non-stick baking paper or Silpat (see Glossary). Place another baking sheet under each.

Put the almond meal and icing sugar in a food processor and process to a fine powder, then sift into a large bowl.

Put the egg whites, caster sugar and powdered egg in a heatproof bowl over a saucepan of simmering water (make sure the base of the bowl doesn't touch the water). Stir gently until the mixture reaches 55–60°C (131–140°F). Remove the bowl and use an electric mixer with a whisk attachment to whisk on medium speed until the egg whites form a shiny firm meringue. Add food colouring (if required). Fold through the almond mixture until combined. Continue to fold the mixture until it falls slowly off the spatula.

Transfer the mixture to a piping (icing) bag with a 7 mm (³⁄₈ inch) plain nozzle. Holding the piping bag about 1.5 cm (⁵⁄₈ inch) above a tray, pipe 3 cm (1¼ inch) rounds on the lined sheets, leaving a 2.5 cm (1 inch) gap between each.

Tap the baking sheets lightly underneath to release any excess air and flatten the macarons. Leave the macarons at room temperature for 30 minutes or until a skin forms. After 10 minutes, preheat the oven to 130°C (250°F/Gas 1). To test if the macarons are ready, gently touch one with your fingertip to check that a light skin has formed — the macarons should not be sticky.

Bake the macarons for 10–12 minutes, until they have a firm outer shell. Remove from the oven and slide the paper with the shells onto wire racks. Cool the macarons completely, then pair them up according to size.

# FRENCH MERINGUE MACARONS

**MAKES 50**

Grease 2 large baking sheets and line with non-stick baking paper or Silpat (see Glossary). Place another baking sheet under each lined baking sheet.

Put the almond meal and icing sugar in a food processor and process to a fine powder, then sift into a large bowl.

Put the egg whites and caster sugar in an electric mixer with a whisk attachment. Whisk on medium speed until the mixture forms stable firm peaks that are soft to touch. Add the food colouring (if required) at this stage. Fold through the almond mixture until the meringue is thick, yet soft enough to fall back into itself.

Transfer the mixture to a piping (icing) bag with a 7 mm (⅜ inch) plain nozzle. Pipe 4 cm (1½ inch) diameter rounds onto the lined baking sheets, leaving a 2.5 cm (1 inch) gap between each macaron.

Tap the baking sheets lightly underneath to release any excess air and flatten the macarons. Leave the macarons at room temperature for 30 minutes or until a skin forms. After 10 minutes, preheat the oven to 130°C (250°F/Gas 1).

To test if the macarons are ready, gently touch one with your fingertip to check that a light skin has formed — the macarons should not be sticky.

Bake the macarons for 10–12 minutes, until they have a firm outer shell. Remove from the oven and slide the paper with the shells onto wire racks. Cool the macarons completely, then pair them up according to size.

*This is the original and most difficult of the macaron methods. The mixture is more delicate so you need to work it perfectly to avoid cracked shells. When you're ready to challenge yourself, test your mettle on the French macaron.*

180 g (6¼ oz) almond meal
180 g (6¼ oz) pure icing (confectioners') sugar
150 g (5½ oz) egg whites, at room temperature
250 g (9 oz) caster (superfine) sugar
Food colouring, if required

**NOTE:** Make sure you leave the egg whites out of the fridge for at least one day or more at room temperature, to let them break down and become acidic. This increases the strength of the protein when whipping.

**101** **BASICS**

# ITALIAN MERINGUE

250 g (9 oz) egg whites
150 g (5½ oz) water
450 g (1 lb) caster
  (superfine) sugar

**USE IN GINGERBREAD HOUSE MACARONS (PAGE 48)**

Put the egg whites in an electric mixer with a whisk attachment. Put the water and sugar in a heavy-based saucepan over medium–low heat and cook, stirring occasionally, until the sugar has dissolved. Brush down the side of the pan with a clean pastry brush dipped in water to avoid any crystallisation. Increase the heat to medium and bring the sugar syrup to 121°C (250°F). With the motor running on medium speed, pour the sugar syrup down the side of the mixer bowl in a slow steady stream. Continue to mix until the temperature drops to 50°C (122°F), stopping the mixer whenever you check the temperature. Use as directed. (Make as needed, as it doesn't store well.)

# CLEAR NEUTRAL GLAZE

250 g (9 oz) water
10 g (¼ oz) pectin NH
  (see Glossary)
265 g (9⅓ oz) caster
  (superfine) sugar
20 g (¾ oz) liquid glucose

**USE IN ST CHOUXMACA (PAGE 86)**

Place the water in a saucepan and bring to 60°C (140°F). Mix the pectin with 65 g (2⅓ oz) of the sugar, add to the water and stir to combine. Bring to the boil and add the remaining sugar. Return to the boil and add the glucose. Remove from the heat and allow to cool completely. Store in an airtight container in the refrigerator. To use, reheat to 35°C (95°F) in a heatproof bowl over a saucepan of simmering water or in the microwave.

# CHOCOLATE CASINGS

## USE IN EASTER EGG YOLK MACARONS (PAGE 55)

300 g (10½ oz) dark couverture chocolate (64%), chopped or buttons

Temper the chocolate (see pages 106–107) and use to fill fifty 2 cm (¾ inch) diameter demisphere flexipan silicone mould cavities. Use a wide chocolate spatula to scrape any excess from the top of the mould sheets in one quick, smooth movement. Tap the sheets on the bench to expel any excess air. Flip each mould sheet over a wide bowl, allowing the excess chocolate to spill into the bowl. Turn the right way up and scrape again with the spatula.

Lay two thin rods (such as chopsticks) parallel on a silicone mat. Turn a mould sheet upside down, laying it on the rods so it doesn't touch the mat. Leave for 1 minute, then turn the right way up and use the spatula to remove the last remnants of excess chocolate. Allow the chocolate to dry for 15 minutes. Repeat with the other mould sheet.

Hold the sheets up to the light — if there are see-through patches you will need to repeat the whole process again (on top of what you have already done). Gently reheat the tempered chocolate by directing a heat gun or hair dryer at the surface, stirring until it is just liquid again.

Fill a piping (icing) bag with a 7 mm (⅜ inch) plain nozzle with the cooled passionfruit gel. Pipe the gel into the chocolate-lined moulds until each is three-quarters full.

Reheat the remaining tempered chocolate with a heat gun or hair dryer until liquid. Fill the top of each mould with chocolate, ensuring they are all sealed completely. Scrape the top with the chocolate scraper, then refrigerate until set.

Pop the chocolates out of the moulds. After piping the ganache onto the macaron shells, gently press a chocolate into the centre of the ganache on each macaron. Top with the remaining shells and continue as instructed on page 55.

# CRÈME PATISSIÈRE

250 g (9 oz) milk
Seeds scraped from
  1 vanilla bean
60 g (2¼ oz) egg yolks
60 g (2¼ oz) caster
  (superfine) sugar
25 g (⁹⁄₁₀ oz) cornflour
  (cornstarch)
100 g (3½ oz) unsalted
  butter, chopped and
  softened slightly

**MAKES ABOUT 480 g (1 lb 1 oz)**

Heat the milk and vanilla seeds in a medium saucepan over medium–low heat until almost boiling. Remove from the heat. Whisk the egg yolks, sugar and cornflour in a bowl until thick and pale. Gradually whisk in the hot milk. Return the mixture to the pan and whisk constantly over medium heat until the custard comes to the boil. Boil for 1 minute. Transfer to a bowl and cover with plastic wrap, pressing it onto the surface to prevent a skin forming. Cool the crème pâtissière to 50°C (122°F), then use a balloon whisk to whisk in the butter until smooth. Cover with plastic wrap as before and refrigerate to cool completely. Before using, use a balloon whisk to whisk until smooth.

# TOASTED PISTACHIO PASTE

250 g (9 oz) pistachio nuts
30 g (1 oz) vegetable oil

Preheat the oven to 180°C (350°F/Gas 4). Line a baking tray with non-stick baking paper. Spread the pistachios over the lined tray and roast for 10–12 minutes or until light golden. Cool slightly, then transfer to a food processor and process to a fine paste. Add up to 30 g (1 oz) oil, with the motor running, if needed.

**VARIATION – PISTACHIO PASTE** Do not toast the nuts. Process to a paste, adding the oil if necessary.

# CITRIC ACID SOLUTION

Put the water in a bowl, add the citric acid and stir until dissolved. Keep in an airtight container in a cool dark place.

10 g (¼ oz) warm water
10 g (¼ oz) citric acid
(see Glossary)

# FRUIT PURÈES

These can be bought from speciality food stores and pastry supply wholesalers, often in Tetrapaks or frozen. Buying them is actually more economical and convenient than making your own, though making them is a simple process. For fruits such as lychee, apricot, cherry, blackcurrant, raspberry, strawberry, mango, peach and mandarin, peel if necessary, then remove any pits, stones or stalks. Process the fruit in a food processor to a purée, then press through a fine sieve (discarding any pulp). You will lose some of the weight of the fruit when sieving it, so keep that in mind when purchasing. Store in the refrigerator or freezer.

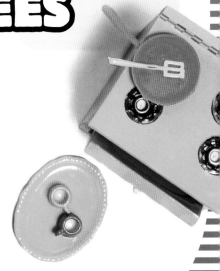

# TEMPERING CHOCOLATE

Tempering is the term used to describe the technique of heating and cooling chocolate to specific temperatures to ensure it sets hard, snaps cleanly when broken and has a professional glossy shine. It also gives the chocolate a higher melting point, which is important when making chocolates and chocolate decorations.

Tempered chocolate is used whenever chocolate is going to be visible in the finished product, such as in Zumbaroni Road (page 91) and Chocarons (page 89). If chocolate is going to be melted and then incorporated into a mixture, there's no need to temper it. You must use couverture chocolate for tempering, and follow the seeding or tabling methods detailed below.

## SEEDING METHOD

500 g (1 lb 2 oz) couverture chocolate (dark, milk or white), chopped or buttons

Melt three-quarters of the chocolate in a clean, dry heatproof bowl over a saucepan of just-simmering water. The water should not touch the base of the bowl. As the chocolate starts to melt, stir gently with a spatula so that the chocolate melts evenly and monitor the temperature with a digital thermometer. When the chocolate reaches 45–48°C (113–118°F) for dark chocolate or 40–45°C (104–113°F) for milk chocolate or white chocolate, remove the bowl from the pan. This is the temperature where the cocoa butter crystals in the chocolate will have melted.

Immediately add the remaining chocolate to the bowl and stir until the temperature drops to 27°C (81°F) and all the pieces of chocolate have melted.

Return the bowl to the saucepan of just-simmering water and reheat the chocolate to its ideal working temperature. This is 31–32°C (88–90°F) for dark chocolate and 29–30°C (84–86°F) for milk chocolate and white chocolate. Stir gently and use the chocolate as soon as it reaches the correct temperature.

To test if the chocolate has been correctly tempered, dip the end of a clean palette knife in it. The chocolate should harden, with no streaks, in approximately 3 minutes. (This is at a room temperature of around 20°C/68°F.)

If the temperature drops while you are working with the tempered chocolate, use a hot-air gun or a hair dryer to gently reheat it to the ideal working temperature.

# TABLING METHOD

You need a marble benchtop for this method.

Melt all the chocolate in a clean, dry heatproof bowl over a saucepan of just-simmering water. The water should not touch the base of the bowl. As the chocolate starts to melt, stir gently with a spatula so that the chocolate melts evenly and monitor the temperature with a digital thermometer. When the chocolate reaches 45–48°C (113–118°F) for dark chocolate or 40–45°C (104–113°F) for milk chocolate or white chocolate, remove the bowl from the pan. This is the temperature where the cocoa butter crystals in the chocolate will have melted.

Pour two-thirds of the chocolate onto the marble and spread out with a large spatula or chocolate scraper. Use the spatula or scraper to push the chocolate into the centre, then spread it out again. Continue until the chocolate thickens slightly.

Scrape the thickened chocolate back into the bowl with the remaining warm chocolate and stir until it reaches 27°C (81°F). Gently heat the chocolate to its ideal working temperature, as listed above.

# TIPS & TRICKS

- Use good-quality ingredients.
- Leave your egg whites out of the fridge for at least a day to break down and become more acidic, as this increases the strength of the protein, creating a more stable foam when whipping. Alternatively, adding 0.5 g (1/50 oz) cream of tartar per 40 g (1½ oz) egg white will give the same result.
- Use clean and dry utensils when whipping eggs.
- Do not over-whisk egg whites. It's better to under-whisk if anything.
- Scrape down the side of the bowl regularly when whisking the macaron mixture to avoid a crust forming. If you don't scrape down the sides, the mixture will dry out very quickly.
- Process the almond meal and icing (confectioners') sugar mixture in a food processor and pass it through a sieve before using. However, take care not to over-process or the mixture will become a paste, as the natural oils will be released from the almonds.
- Always fold ingredients in well.
- Be careful when folding the macaron mixture to work the air out, as this is a key element and can make or break the mixture.
- Non-stick baking paper or Silpat (see Glossary) is necessary to line your baking trays. You cannot use greaseproof paper or pipe directly onto the trays, even if they are of the non-stick variety.
- Use completely flat baking trays (known as baking sheets) to ensure an even airflow around the macaron shells.
- When piping, leave a space of about 2.5 cm (1 inch) on either side of each macaron to allow the air to flow around them evenly.
- After piping, depending on the consistency of your mixture, remember to tap the tray to release any excess air bubbles and give the macarons a smooth, flat surface.
- Always let the macarons sit before baking to develop a skin and ensure they are dry to touch before putting them in the oven.
- Bake macarons on double baking sheets, as this filters the direct heat to the bottom of the tray, resulting in more gentle, consistent cooking.
- Bake a small test batch of macarons to check your oven. This will let you see what happens during the baking stage so you can make any adjustments that may be necessary for your oven. All ovens are different, so it's important to know how your oven performs.

- When checking if the macaron shells are ready, just grab one with two fingers and give it a slight jiggle — it should move slightly, but be quite stable to touch.
- Always cool macaron shells completely before trying to remove them from the baking paper, as they can collapse or still be sticking a little before this.
- When pairing up the macaron shells, transfer them to a tray lined with non-stick baking paper first. This will keep them clean and ensure they can be easily moved if required.
- Make sure that you pair up cooled macaron shells according to size before filling them. This will result in beautiful zumbarons with a consistent appearance.
- If you are using a Thermomix to make a ganache filling, put all the ingredients inside and set to 50°C (122°F). For a custriano, put all the ingredients inside and set to 100°C (212°F). Follow the specific recipes to incorporate the butter into the cooled custriano.
- When filling the macaron shells, be generous if there is just one component. If there is a second component to place in the centre, allow room for this when applying the first component as this will make it expand.
- Sometimes you may have more or less ganache than you need to fill the full quantity of macarons. It's better to fill each macaron properly and have a few shells or ganache left over, rather than under- or over-filling the macarons.
- When your zumbarons are sandwiched there should be 4–5 mm (⅙–¼ inch) of filling between the two shells. It should look juicy, a bit like a little hamburger.
- Make sure that when you sandwich the zumbarons you push down firmly so the filling pushes out until it is flush with the edge of the macaron shells.
- Place the finished zumbarons on a covered tray in the refrigerator for 24 hours to obtain the optimum texture for eating. During this time, the macaron shells will absorb some of the moisture from the filling, which will soften them slightly. The shells should not be soggy after this stage.
- Zumbarons are best stored, covered, at room temperature for up to 2 days. They can also be kept, covered, in the fridge for 3–4 days, depending on the filling. If your zumbarons are not going to be eaten within a few days, it's best to freeze them, in an airtight container or on a plate, covered with plastic wrap.

# TROUBLESHOOTING

## 1. MACARON SHELLS CRACK DURING BAKING

There are three possible explanations for this. Firstly, if the macaron shells haven't formed a skin before baking it is likely they will crack when the water content from the macaron mixture evaporates and turns to steam. If there is no skin to prevent the steam escaping it will just explode from the top, cracking the surface. Secondly, your oven temperature may be too high. Finally, sometimes textures such as sugar, salts and flours that are sprinkled or dusted over the macaron shells can cause them to crack.

## 2. EGG WHITES WON'T WHIP

There may be too much fat in the egg whites. The fat can be traces of egg yolk or grease from a bowl or beaters that are not totally clean. Water will also inhibit the egg whites' ability to whip up, so you need to ensure all utensils are clean and dry.

## 3. MACARON MIXTURE IS TOO LIQUID

Either the egg whites were whisked on too high a speed, so they didn't create enough strength and therefore deflated when the other ingredients were mixed in, or the egg whites were over-whisked and as they dried out they become weak and then collapsed when other ingredients were mixed in.

## 4. MACARON MIXTURE IS TOO THICK

One reason can be that the ingredients were too cold. For example, when making Italian meringue the mixture has to be 50°C (122°F) when the dry ingredients are added to allow you to get the correct consistency. Other explanations could be over-whisking the meringue mixture or weighing the ingredients incorrectly.

## 5. UNCOOKED MACARON SHELLS WON'T FORM A SKIN

Air temperature and humidity are the main culprits here, so make sure the kitchen is cool and dry. If it isn't, move the macaron shells to a room that is. Excess moisture in the macaron mixture will also prevent the shells from getting a skin.

## 6. MACARON SHELLS DON'T HAVE A 'FOOT'

The macaron shells didn't form a proper skin before baking. The skin needs to be dry to the touch in order to achieve a good 'foot'. A mixture that is too runny or an oven temperature that is too high can also contribute to a lack of 'foot'.

## 7. MACARON SHELLS HAVE AIR POCKETS

This is the result of oven temperature. If it is too high or too low, the mixture will bake prematurely or may collapse during cooking. A temperature of 135°C (275°F/Gas 1) is a good base for baking macaron shells.

## 8. MACARON SHELLS STICK TO BAKING PAPER OR SILPAT

If you prefer to cool macarons on the lined baking sheets (rather than transferring them, still on the paper, to wire racks), cook them for a little less time as the residual heat from the trays will continue to cook the macarons. Remove the lower trays before leaving the macarons to cool.

## 9. MACARON SHELLS HAVE NOT COLOURED EVENLY

This is due to the oven being too hot or hot spots in your oven, which can result in uneven baking.

## 10. MACARON SHELLS ARE UNDER-COOKED

This is usually due to them being taken out of the oven prematurely or setting the oven temperature too low. Always preheat the oven properly and to the correct setting, and check that your macaron shells are cooked before taking them out of the oven. They should have a firm outer shell and the base should feel dry — they should not be sticky. Importantly, get to know your oven and its correct temperature for baking certain products. Another reason can be too much moisture in the macaron mixture, which will retard the cooking process and lengthen the time necessary to bake the shells. If your macaron mixture doesn't look right, start again.

## 11. MACARON SHELLS ARE OVER-COOKED

This is simply because they have spent too long in the oven. When they are ready the shells should have a slight wobble, but be firm enough not to move.

## 12. HOW TO SAVE OVER-COOKED MACARON SHELLS

Crisp and biscuit-like macaron shells can be improved by sandwiching with a filling that has a fairly high moisture content (such as fruit curds and those with jelly or jam inserts), then refrigerating, uncovered, for 2–3 days so that the moisture from the filling, as well as the air in the refrigerator, will be absorbed by the shells and bring them to the right texture.

## 13. ZUMBARONS ARE SOGGY

There are two reasons for this. Firstly, they may have spent too much time, uncovered, in the refrigerator where there is too much moisture in the air. Secondly, if there is too much moisture or water content in the filling, the macaron shell may have absorbed too much moisture (the shells have a high sugar content and sugar draws moisture from its surroundings easily).

## 14. ZUMBARONS ARE BECOMING STALE OR DRYING OUT QUICKLY

Check that they are stored in an airtight environment in a cool dry place (around 21°C/70°F). If it is hot, store them, covered, in the refrigerator to keep them cool and prevent them spoiling.

# GLOSSARY

**ALMOND MILK** is available from supermarkets and health food stores.

**BERGAMOT ESSENTIAL OIL** is available from health food stores.

**CITRIC ACID** is available from supermarkets.

**COCOA BUTTER & COCOA MASS:** when cocoa beans are cleaned and separated from their shells, cocoa nibs (the edible part of the bean) are produced. The nibs are then roasted, crushed and processed into premium-quality cocoa mass, cocoa butter or cocoa powder. *Cocoa mass* is the most important ingredient in the manufacture of chocolate. *Cocoa butter* is solid and has no taste, but it helps produce shine and gives harder cracking properties to tempered chocolate. Available from speciality food stores, speciality pastry suppliers and online.

**DATE MOLASSES** is available from Middle Eastern grocery stores.

**EDIBLE SILVER METALLIC** is available from cake decorating stores.

**EUCALYPTUS OIL** is available from health food stores and some supermarkets.

**FREEZE-DRIED BEETROOT POWDER** is sold at speciality food stores and pastry suppliers.

**GELATINE LEAVES** are available in different strengths so instead of stating the number of leaves to use we have given gram measurements so you can adapt the recipes for the various types of leaf gelatine available. They are sold at speciality food stores.

**GELLAN** is a gelling agent obtained from the fermentation of *Sphingomonas elodea* bacteria. It is available from selected speciality food stores and online.

**GIANDUJA CHOCOLATE** is a chocolate and hazelnut paste, available from speciality food stores.

**INVERTED SUGAR** is a syrup made by heating and adding an acid (such as citric acid) to a simple sugar syrup. It retains moisture, so is used in baked goods to help prevent them drying out. As it doesn't crystallise, it is also helpful to prevent ice crystals forming in ice creams, sorbets and glazes. It is available from speciality pastry suppliers.

**IOTA** is a gelling agent extracted from a type of red algae found on the coasts of the north Atlantic, as well as in the Philippine and Indonesian seas. It is available from selected speciality food stores and online.

**ISOMALT** is a sugar made from the natural sugar in beetroot and has half the kilojoules of cane sugar. Unlike regular sucrose, it can be heated up to 190°C (375°F) without changing colour and can be used to create virtually any shape. It is available from speciality pastry suppliers and online.

**JAPANESE MAYONNAISE** has a unique taste that goes particularly well with Japanese flavours. It is available from Asian grocers and some supermarkets.

**KAPPA** (full name kappa carrageenan) is a natural gelling agent made from red seaweed that thickens and stabilises. It is available from speciality food stores and pastry suppliers.

**KUMABO COUVERTURE CHOCOLATE** is a bitter, extremely dark chocolate with an 80% cocoa solid content, available from speciality food stores.

**PANDAN LEAVES AND EXTRACT** are taken from an aromatic member of the pandanus family and are widely used in Asian cooking. The leaves are long and thin. Available from Asian grocers.

**PECTIN** is a natural product that can be found in the cell wall of all plants. Most commercial pectin is extracted under mildly acidic conditions from citrus peel or apple pomace (the pulp that is left after apples are squeezed and juiced). There are a number of pectins available, all with specific characteristics. *Yellow pectin*, also called pectin jaune, and *pectin NH* are available from speciality pastry suppliers and online.

**POPROCKS** are available from speciality pastry suppliers and some lolly (candy) shops. Be sure to buy the plain variety, not the flavoured ones.

**POWDERED EGG WHITE** is available at speciality food stores.

**SILPAT** is a non-stick baking mat made of fibreglass and silicone that is available from speciality kitchen stores and online.

**SODASTREAM FLAVOURS** (cola and sugar-free cola) are available from supermarkets.

**TONKA BEANS** are native to South America and are used in a similar way to a vanilla bean, however the beans are finely grated like nutmeg. Only a little is used as tonka beans contain coumarin, which is an anti-coagulant and in high doses can thin out the blood to dangerous levels. They are available from speciality spice stores and online.

**UHT COCONUT CREAM** is available from selected Asian grocers. (The Kara brand is nearly all coconut, so I find it gives the best results.)

**WASABI POWDER** is available from Asian grocers.

**WASABI SESAME SEEDS** are available from Japanese grocers and online.

**XANTHAN GUM** is produced by fermenting corn starch and is used extensively as a thickener. It is gluten free and available from health food stores and selected supermarkets.

# INDEX

Published in 2012 by Murdoch Books, an imprint of Allen & Unwin

Murdoch Books Australia
83 Alexander Street
Crows Nest NSW 2065
Phone: +61 (0) 2 8425 0100
Fax: +61 (0) 2 9906 2218
www.murdochbooks.com.au
info@murdochbooks.com.au

Murdoch Books UK
Erico House, 6th Floor
93–99 Upper Richmond Road
Putney, London SW15 2TG
Phone: +44 (0) 20 8785 5995
www.murdochbooks.co.uk
info@murdochbooks.co.uk

For Corporate Orders & Custom Publishing contact Noel Hammond,
National Business Development Manager Murdoch Books Australia

Publisher: Sally Webb
Designer: Tania Gomes
Photographer: Cath Muscat
Stylist: Vanessa Colyer Tay
Project Editor: Alice Grundy
Editor: Anna Scobie
Food Editor: Lucy Nunes
Home Economist: Grace Campbell
Production: Karen Small

A cataloguing-in-publication entry is available from the catalogue
of the National Library of Australia at www.nla.gov.au.

A catalogue record for this book is available from the British Library.

Printed by 1010 Printing International Limited, China. Reprinted 2012, 2015.

The publisher and stylist would like to thank Venucci, Have You Met Miss Jones,
Koskela, Luxxbox and Paper Eskimo for lending equipment for use and photography
and Joseph Gardner Sgro, Alenka von Engelhardt and Kate Holcombe for providing
styling assistance.

IMPORTANT: Those who might be at risk from the effects of salmonella poisoning
(the elderly, pregnant women, young children and those suffering from immune
deficiency diseases) should consult their doctor with any concerns about eating
raw eggs.

OVEN GUIDE: You may find cooking times vary depending on the oven you are
using. For fan-forced ovens, as a general rule, set the oven temperature to 20°C
(35°F) lower than indicated in the recipe.

We have used 20 ml (4 teaspoon) tablespoon measures. If you are using a 15 ml
(3 teaspoon) tablespoon add an extra teaspoon of the ingredient for each
tablespoon specified.